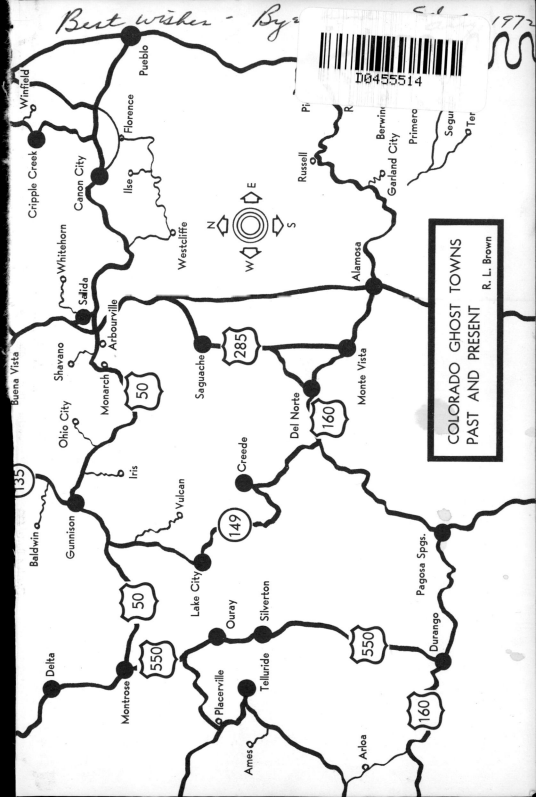

Best wishes - Bye... ...1972

COLORADO GHOST TOWNS
PAST AND PRESENT

R. L. Brown

COLORADO GHOST TOWNS—
PAST AND PRESENT

COLORADO GHOST TOWNS —
PAST and PRESENT

By

ROBERT L. BROWN

ILLUSTRATED WITH PHOTOGRAPHS

THE CAXTON PRINTERS, LTD.
CALDWELL, IDAHO
1972

Standard Book Number 0-87004-218-1

Library of Congress Catalog Card No. 77-140121

Lithographed and bound in the United States of America by
The CAXTON PRINTERS, Ltd.
Caldwell, Idaho 83605
115819

For
Freda and Francis B. Rizzari

PREFATORY NOTE

EACH TOWN INCLUDED in this book was selected on the basis of three questions. First, was its history interesting, quaint, or unusual? Second, are early photographs of the town in its heyday still available? Third, what is the present status of its site? Frequently, the answer to this last question is that the buildings are gone and their locations are in the process of returning to their natural state. For this reason, location of the site would have been virtually impossible without recourse to early photographs.

In examining the work of 19th century photographers, it appears that most used wide-angle optics on their wet plate view cameras. To match their shots for this book with today's 35mm camera, lenses of 35mm and 28mm were needed more frequently than regular optics. Only two pictures, those of London Junction and Tabasco, required the use of telephotos. Panatomic X was the only film used, and a green filter was occasionally employed.

Of the problems encountered in compiling a book of this sort, the most persistent is the separation of fact from fiction. One account, for example, records that the opening of a mountain trail required 400 men and 600 oxen. These are preposterous figures—perhaps 50 men and a dozen yoke of oxen were used for this purpose. It has been this historian's task to seek out the truth in every case possible. When the facts contained in extant sources varied widely, every effort was made to discover authentic corroborations. At no time, however, has unverifiable material been included. Nevertheless, if error has at any time crept into the work, the author apologizes in advance.

R. L. B.

&

ACKNOWLEDGMENTS

IN THE EXTENDED PROCESS of preparing any book one incurs many debts. Several words of special gratitude are due my wife Evelyn, and our two children, Diana and Marshall, for their patience during many long trips to remote locations, and for their help in identification of photographic angles. Berta and Bill Anderson hiked through countless miles of Colorado's back country with us.

My thanks also to Jennie Ives and Bonnie Sedustine who did much of the preliminary typing, and to my wife Evelyn for typing the final manuscript. Freda and Francis B. Rizzari gave generously of their time, patience, skill, and understanding by proofreading the completed manuscript for errors and omissions. Virginia McConnell checked the historical accuracy of my chapter on Balfour. Arthur Abe and Marshall Brown assisted with technical photographic items. Many of the old pictures came from the fine collections of Richard A. Ronzio, Francis B. Rizzari, the late Carl Mathews, Jane and Louis Bass, Mrs. Dean Ives, Mrs. Bert Johnson, the late Elizabeth Roller, Velma Churchill, Mae Bertagnoli and Mrs. Merill C. Cross. The photographic library of the State Historical Society of Colorado and the Western History Collection of the Denver Public Library filled a number of other photographic needs with rare old pictures. Some others came from the Rio Grande Archives and from the superb collection of Fred and Jo Mazzulla.

Jack and Erma Morison, L. G. McKee, Carl Mathews, Mrs.

Mary Lou Miles, Elizabeth Roller, Rose and Quentin Sagrillo and many others furnished me with information by letters, tape recordings and in personal interviews. Mrs. Enid Thompson, Mrs. Kay Pearson, Mrs. Laura Ekstrom and Mrs. Louisa Ward Arps spent hours filling my numerous requests and were of tremendous assistance in researching information at the Library of the State Historical Society of Colorado. Mrs. Alys Freeze and her fine staff at the Western History Collection, Denver Public Library, also devoted a great deal of time to finding answers to often obscure questions. Mrs. Opal Harber, Mrs. Hazel Lundberg and Mr. James Davis were particularly helpful.

The following references listed in alphabetical order were used in the preparation of this book. The *Apex Pine Cone* for July 15, 1899; M. Beshoar, *All About Trinidad* (Denver, Times Steam Printing House and Blank Book Manufactury, 1882); Edward T. Bollinger, *Rails that Climb*, Santa Fe, 1950; *Camp and Plant* magazine for January 11, March 8, and June 2, 1902, and April 9, 1904; the *Central City Register-Call* for November 17, 1886; the Colorado Business Directory, all volumes through 1905; the *Colorado Miner* for January 25, 1872, March 26, 1874, January 16, 1875, December 29, 1877 and March 1, 1884; the *Denver Daily News* for March 16, 1899; the *Denver Republican* for January 19, 1889, October 26, 1890, September 9, 1897, May 4, 1900, May 25, 1902, November 16, 1904, September 29, 1905, March 16 and 17, and June 22, 1906 and November 5, 1911; the *Denver Times* for July 8, 1897, February 13, November 14, 15, and 18, December 15 and 31, 1898, February 6, March 8, April 9 and 19, May 11, 23, and 31, July 7, October 15, and December 31, 1899, January 24, March 14, July 31, October 3, December 2 and 30, 1900, March 3, 12, and 22, April 26, and 29, June 9 and 10, September 28, and October 13, 1901; Perry Eberhart, *Guide to the Colorado Ghost Towns and Mining Camps* (Denver, Sage Books, 1959); the Denver Post for April 15 and November 30, 1897, October 15, 1899, Oc-

tober 13, 1901, January 30, 1903 and April 23, 1956; Frank
Fossett, *Colorado, Its Gold and Silver Mines* (New York:
C. J. Crawford, Printer and Stationer, 1880); Don and Jean
Griswold and Fred and Jo Mazzulla *Colorado's Century of
Cities,* published by the authors (Denver: 1958); Frank Hall,
History of Colorado, four volumes published between 1889
and 1895 by the Blakely Printing Company of Chicago; Vir-
ginia McConnell, *Bayou Salado* (Denver, Colorado, Sage
Books, 1966); the *Pueblo Chieftain* for February 2, 1965; the
Rocky Mountain News for July 30, 1866, March 21 and July
21, 1872, December 2, 1874, June 1 and September 26, 1885,
September 24, 1896, March 30 and July 21, 1899, March 12,
1905, August 4, 1946, April 20, 1950, January 27, 1952,
October 13, 1954 and March 11, 1956; the *Salida Daily Mail*
for June 11, 1956 and October 27, 1957; Marshall Sprague,
The Great Gates (Little, Brown and Company, Boston,
1964); *Trail and Timberline* magazine (The Colorado Mountain Club, Denver, complete file); Frank Waters, *Midas of
the Rockies* (Denver, the University of Denver Press, 1949);
and last but far from least Muriel Sibell Wolle's magnificent
and monumental *Stampede to Timberline* (Boulder, the author, 1949).

&

INTRODUCTION

In 1893 Frederick Jackson Turner, a professor at the University of Wisconsin, put forth a hypothesis to aid in a clearer understanding of the various migrations and historical developments which opened the western frontier. Turner called his thesis "The Significance of the Frontier in American History." In it he attempted to interpret frontier characteristics in terms of the geographical environment. He theorized that the untamed land forced a series of mild social revolutions on each successive frontier, resulting in a freer, more self-reliant, and therefore truly democratic society. Those persons who could not adapt fell by the wayside. Those who made the adjustment to their new environment became a hardier breed and the progenitors of a people who were more distinctly individual and therefore American.

One writer described the end product of Turner's theory as "men with the bark on." Each successive society supposedly built upon the experiences of former frontiers. Democracy emerged not from the founding fathers, according to professor Turner, but from the frontier. While some contemporary historians question the Turner thesis, others defend it with an almost religious zeal. For the student of the American West, however, Turner's writings still stand as a pioneer attempt to interpret the enormous void that existed between the culture, way of life, and state of mind of the individualistic westerner as compared with his eastern cousin.

For whatever reasons, life in the west, and particularly in the mining towns, was more glandular than in the rest of the nation. Most argonauts carried an atmosphere of the western landscape with them, an awareness of open prairies as limitless as time, of huge snow-capped primeval mountains, and of mineralized hillsides filled with miners and mules. Most were guided by 19th century Victorian consciences that reflected the ever-present conflict between a fine old fashioned sense of sin and the realities of their new surroundings. There was a lingering enchantment with violence and a compulsion for quick and final physical showdowns.

Everyday contacts with brutal and harsh conditions gave some men an attitude of callous indifference toward law enforcement and crime generally. In Colorado's early-day towns only three classifications of crimes were recognized. For less serious offenses the miscreant was subjected to public whipping. More comprehensive offenses against good taste could result in banishment from the district. Crimes such as murder or theft of a horse were punished by hanging. In all instances the punishment reflected the pioneer reluctance to spend money on law-enforcement officials or the construction of jails. If nothing else, the punishments meted out were economical.

And of course the Indians lived here too and some cultural conflict with them was inevitable. Where formerly an occasional traveler or caravan had crossed Indian country, now there were many. Few of these people respected the rights of the red man. Many activities of the new intruders gave them cause for alarm. Not only were stage roads built through their country, but railroads also came in great numbers after the Civil War. Both military posts and stage stations were established, and claims of homesteaders and miners were validated at the Indian's expense. With little regard for long-established hunting ranges, the earth was torn up, game was driven off, towns were established and the aborigine was herded onto a reservation. At one point a thoroughly aroused

Chief Red Cloud exhorted his people about their future, saying, "if the 'white eyes' are not stopped now, one day we will wake up to find that he has built his ugly privies all the way to the western ocean."

Despite the Indian uprisings of the 1860s and 70s, organized raids on established towns were rare. Indians did sack and burn Julesburg, and they once attacked Fort Sedgwick, Colorado City and one of the early villages in the Leadville area. Raids on outlying farms, however, were more successful and less dangerous. Indians successfully attacked settlers on Plum Creek, in the Cache La Poudre, Arkansas, and South Platte Valleys. But in general Indian efforts suffered from both lack of coordination and a failure of the tribes to cooperate. Contemporary fiction to the contrary, the red man won far more battles than he lost. What the Sioux did to Custer or Fetterman was much more typical than the action of Chivington against the Cheyenne at Sand Creek. With the end of the Civil War, no force on earth could have withstood for long the numbers of troops who were now free to fight in the west. The Indian lost his last battles and the rest is history.

Gold in Colorado awakened many depression-ridden Americans to new opportunities for adventure in the west. Quite suddenly, thousands of impoverished people found themselves rushing to the Rockies for gold. The Anglo-Saxon population of Colorado grew from a handful of trappers in 1858 to about 25,242 souls when Governor William Gilpin took the first head count in 1861, and men outnumbered women by 30 to one.

By that time the rush was on. Most of the gold seekers came overland, crossing the Great Plains, facing countless natural hazards along with the ever-present danger from hostile Indians. A few came by sea, tolerating the boredom of the nearly six months' voyage around South America to San Francisco, then overland to Denver.

Over the years, those who became rich often did so by living off the miners. Many fortunes were made by persons who never sank a pick into a quartz vein. Among them were storekeepers, gamblers, traders, road builders, mine speculators, painted ladies, barkeepers, pack train and stagecoach operators, railroad builders and hotel proprietors. Sadly, only a few miners ever hit pay dirt in large quantities.

In common with other western mineral rushes, Colorado's came on the heels of an economic depression; in this case it was the panic of 1857. During hard times people view the discovery of gold in a different light, and a rush results. If gold is found in good times, the news causes scarcely a ripple. One example will suffice.

Zebulon Montgomery Pike met James Purcell, a trapper in Santa Fe during the winter of 1807. Purcell told of having found gold in South Park in 1805. When Pike's journal was published, no rush occurred. However, South Park was thoroughly prospected during the two decades after 1859.

Colorado's mining frontier was also influenced by another great national calamity. It opened on the eve of the Civil War and suffered a collapse between 1861 and 1865. With only a few exceptions, the mines were kept open by standby crews. Little in the way of precious metal was produced. After the surrender at Appomattox the boom was on again.

With peace came massive unemployment, and fresh new stories and rumors of discovery became prevalent. A new rush of prospectors from California, the Mississippi Valley and elsewhere, headed for Colorado and populated the region within the next decade. And wherever rich mines were found, clusters of satellite towns mushroomed into existence. Many adopted picturesque names like Gold Hill, Tin Cup, Holy Cross City, North Star, and Silver Creek. But the towns themselves were hardly picturesque. In the beginning most consisted of rude assortments of dugouts and frame shanties, scattered in disorder over the gulches and hillsides. Quantities of canvas tents, log cabins with blanket walls, brush roofs, and potato sack doors and windows, could be seen. Old skirts and other discarded clothing were used to fill cracks and keep out the cold. Old liquor barrels became chimneys for these smoking open-fronted hovels of dirt and rock.

Three important and distinct periods occurred in the life cycle of most mining camps. First of all, following the original discovery, came placer mining and development work on the various claims. This phase usually lasted from two to five years. Next came the gradual transition to deep mining as the placer gravels were stripped. Mining beneath the surface required capital, something most miners lacked. Hence outside financial help was recruited in the east or from Europe. Sometimes hydraulic mining occurred in this second period. Finally, if the gold or silver still persisted in paying quantities, came corporate business organization of the claims. In the process many of the original prospectors were dispossessed and ended up working for the corporations.

Most of the early towns were filthy. In the absence of sanitation departments, refuse from butcher shops and all manner of garbage and waste was thrown into the streets. Herds of cattle and dozens of dimly-domesticated horses and mules added to the problem. Personal cleanliness was little better. Few people bothered to bathe. Most slept in their clothes, and as winter approached, new thicknesses of shirts and pants were added to keep out the cold. With the approach of summer they were removed, layer by layer. As a consequence, epidemics swept the towns and old diaries are replete with complaints of dysentery, diarrhea, assorted infections, and bizarre skin disorders. Only their location at high altitudes, where chill nights retarded bacteria growth, kept some towns from being virtual pest houses.

When families began to arrive in later migrations, most towns settled down, cleaned up and rebuilt. Quite a number became pleasant, clean and rather sophisticated little villages. Some, with different economic bases, have survived and enjoy permanent populations in the present century. But many of the others became ghost towns when their mines stopped producing, when the Sherman Act was repealed in 1893, when railroads were abandoned, when shipping costs for ore devoured the profits, when the towns were destroyed by fires and snowslides, or when the west declined temporarily as a consequence of the general mining collapse.

Under these conditions most of the places we now call ghost towns were born, and died. Many were tacked up on the steep mountainsides, fully expecting the brief, rugged existences which characterized their short life cycles. Others, like Georgetown, were constructed as homesick reminders of New England or Cornwall villages, assimilated into the rugged cliffs or above timberline tundra of Colorado's Rockies.

In all, Colorado has about 700 of these authentic ghost towns, founded during the mining period. Many still exist, scattered along the back-country byways or nestled in the solitude of their high mountain valleys. This book has been prepared for the person who enjoys browsing among the scenes of History's colorful yesterdays. However, a note of caution is appropriate at this point. In visiting an abandoned town, keep in mind that the old buildings are both fragile and tinder dry. A thoughtlessly discarded cigaret or match, an abandoned campfire, or careless acts of vandalism may destroy these historic places forever.

$\wp$

TABLE OF CONTENTS

LIST OF ILLUSTRATIONS

COLORADO GHOST TOWNS—
PAST AND PRESENT

1.

AMES

WHEN GEORGE CROFUTT's *Grip-Sack Guide of Colorado* was first published in 1881, there was no mention of Ames within its voluminous roster of Colorado communities. Four years later his updated 1885 edition had rolled off the presses in Omaha. By this time Ames was booming and consequently rated four whole lines in the terse Crofutt style.

Chronologically, life had started at Ames during the summer of 1881 when Otto Mears constructed a 60-mile-long toll road to the site from Sargents. Just what the factors were that motivated the visionary Mears in this undertaking, history does not record. The construction of a settlement here began in 1882 when a smelting works was erected beside the rushing San Miguel River. When the word got out, some 200 people, measured by the 19th century penchant for round numbers, showed up for work and started building a nucleus of houses around the smelter.

To serve the new community, and others in its vicinity, a thrice weekly stagecoach service came in from Placerville, 18 miles away. Despite the boom and mercurial growth of near-by Telluride, the town of Montrose, far to the north, remained the principal outfitting point for Ames throughout the 80s. When the smelter closed, life at the town underwent a radical change and prosperity came to a grinding halt.

Actually, several factors contributed to the failure of the smelting enterprise. Although there were many successful mines in the neighborhood, none of them was actually at

Ames. The fabulously successful Gold King Property, for example, was at an altitude of 12,000 feet, while Ames was at the very bottom of the deep, sheer-walled canyon. High transportation costs devoured the profits. A second factor was the growth of the more advantageously located town of Ophir, just 3 miles away. A railroad connection might have saved the day, but the Rio Grande Southern did not reach the town until 1890, when the ill-fated smelter was little more than a memory.

Ames acquired its second lease on life largely because of the dream of a somewhat unusual man. Allegedly, L. L. Nunn made his first financial mark in life by installing a bathtub in his house. Word of this wonderful facility soon leaked out to the men employed in the nearby mines. For a sliding scale fee that sometimes reached $1.00 a head, miners on their way to "see the elephant" in Telluride could stop at the Nunn homestead for a much-needed bath. By profession Nunn was an attorney, hired to represent the owners of the rich Gold King property above Alta. Profits, it seems, were dwindling due to exhorbitant fuel costs. With foreclosure and loss of their investments imminent, the stockholders engaged the attorney to seek a way out of their difficulties.

For a lawyer, his approach was most unconventional. Why not, he reasoned, trim expenses by harnessing the power of the swift-running San Miguel River? To make a long story short, Nunn built a power plant at Ames, changed the economic base of the town, and saved the day for his clients. The Nunn idea resulted in the first commercial transmission of high pressure electricity in history.

Using some of the same techniques and avenues of information that had helped to popularize his bathtub caper, word of the newest Nunn achievement soon reached other mining camps. Almost inevitably, a demand for expanded services followed. Perhaps the most imaginative of his ventures was the one that resulted in the extension of his transmission lines across the lofty and beautiful Imogene Pass, more than 13,000

Collection of Rose and Quentin Sagrillo
Ames, showing the power station and some of the homes

Collection of Robert L. Brown
The Ames power station in 1969

feet high. There, on the Ouray side of the range, power from the little plant at Ames was used at the great Camp Bird, Revenue, and other properties near Sneffels.

There's still a power plant at Ames, generating electricity for a variety of nearby projects, but the town's appearance has changed greatly since the early days. To see it, take U.S. Highway 550 north from Ouray or south from Montrose to Ridgway. You might pause here and go one block off the main street to see the movie set. Among others, "How the West Was Won" and a recent John Wayne film were made here. At this writing the simulated false-fronts and other pseudo-western structures are still standing.

From Ridgway, drive west on the newly surfaced Highway 62 to Placerville. Cross the bridge and turn southeast on State Highway 145 to a point about two miles north of Telluride. Go south here and follow the highway to Ophir. For persons traveling in this direction, the Ames road is unmarked. The easiest way is to go into Ophir, turn around and backtrack along the highway as it traverses the curving landfill for about a quarter of a mile to the Ames sign, visible from this direction only.

Turn left here on the graded road that drops sharply down to the bottom of the canyon. Total distance on this road is under two miles. Here, still nestled beside the river is the tiny village of Ames.

2.

ARBOURVILLE

FOR SHEER CONFUSION of names, few Colorado communities can surpass Arbourville. At various times its name has been spelled as Aberville, Arbour Ville, Arboursville, Arbor Villa and Arbourville. Two versions seem to have survived with regard to the origin of the town's name. In one of these, it came from the fact that the cabins were set in among a virtual arbor of aspen and evergreen trees. In the other, we hear that a man named Aber or Arbour came up with friends from Silver Cliff to take their place among the earliest settlers here. Allegedly, upwards of 100 lots were sold during the first day. In any case, a contemporary newspaper account reported that many cabins were under construction on July 31, 1879. By 1885, there were 150 people living there.

Arbourville probably survived largely because of its fortunate location, high up on the eastern slope of lofty Monarch Pass, and very close to this important artery. Within the period of years during which the mining fever lasted, Arbourville was within the Monarch Mining District. In his 1885 edition of the *Grip-Sack Guide of Colorado,* George Crofutt noted that the principal occupations at Arbourville were mining and stock raising. Actually, few mineral properties of any import were adjacent to Arbourville. While some miners did reside here, for the most part they commuted to their work at the mines around Monarch, a few miles farther up the mountain. Some of the other men worked at the

Arbourville smelter, treating and refining the ores that had been shipped in from several of the other Monarch District properties.

In addition to the several private homes, Arbourville had a hotel, a boardinghouse, post office, general store and a stagecoach station. Of great importance in that early pre-railroad era, regular stagecoach service was available from Salida through Maysville, Junction City (Garfield), Arbourville and Monarch (Chaffee City). Measured by the standards of its time, these passenger and commerce carriers fulfilled a genuine social need, maintaining contact between these isolated settlements. The fare from Maysville to Arbourville, five miles away was 50¢.

During the 1880s, Arbourville became the great Saturday night social center for unmarried miners from all over the Monarch District. If contemporary speculations were at all correct, the reason for this popularity was the fact that Arbourville had the only brothel in the entire area; a large, well-run and remarkably endowed institution for its day. Expressed in the broadest terms, this love store was the biggest business in the town. One waggish newspaper reporter made the succinct observation that Arbourville had failed to show progress in comparison with its neighboring towns because it was content to let life revolve around the sociological norms of its parlor house.

In more recent times, the story of Arbourville has become inextricably entwined with the life of the late Frank Gimlett, the so-called hermit of Arbor-Villa (his spelling). Long after the town was deserted by others, Gimlett stayed on, charming tourists with his spicy and unlikely versions of life in the old days. And in the long stretches of winter, when few visitors came up the mountain, Gimlett passed his time by writing. Nine softbound volumes called *Over Trails of Yesterday* were produced. They sold for 25¢ each and contained stories and accounts of life at Junction City, Monarch, Whitepine, etc. Additionally, they contained much of the "Hermit's" own philosophy particularly his diatribes upon the futility of women.

Although the themes rarely changed, the titles did. Under such names as "Modern Women Found Wanting in a Christian World," or "The Futility of Loving Vagarious Woman," Gimlett allowed others to share his thinking. At times his writing seems to have reached a fairly wide audience. Once he got a long protest letter from Rep. Clare Boothe Luce in defense of her sex. Frank Gimlett must have had some wonderful tongue-in-cheek interludes, because despite popular conceptions of hermits and despite his writing, Gimlett had long ago taken the plunge overboard into emotional waters and his wife lived there secretly with him at "Arbor-Villa," as he called it.

To pass the long winter nights, the "Hermit" wrote long epistles to the Congress in Washington, to the Secretary of the Treasury, and the President, F. D. Roosevelt, who once sent an answer. During one particularly arduous winter Gimlett set himself up as guardian of all the ice and snow on the nearby mountains. Filled with gargantuan optimism, he totaled up the time sheet and fired off a bill for $50,000 to Washington, claiming that not one shovelful of snow had ever been stolen during all of the years since he had started guarding it.

Gimlett is perhaps best remembered for the project that occupied much of his time during his declining years. Here in Colorado we have hundreds of un-named peaks, huge, towering summits that have never been graced with any official designation. Two such mountains, a beautifully rounded and quite well-matched pair, dominate the horizon near Monarch Pass, just west of Arbourville. Following a period of prolonged meditation, the "Hermit" decided that these mountains bore a distinct resemblance to certain physiological aspects of his favorite motion picture actress. From this mountain stronghold a veritable barrage of letters began to devolve upon Washington officialdom, suggesting, even insisting, that these aesthetically pleasing domes be officially designated as the Ginger Peaks. With high good humor, the natives adopted the name and refer to them as the Ginger Peaks even today. Washington, however, has never acted to make it official. When Gimlett was laid to rest a few years ago a lot of color and individuality passed from the local scene. The folklore of the county was undoubtedly much enriched because he passed this way.

Several buildings below the highway mark the site of Arbourville today. To see them, drive west from Poncha Springs on U.S. Highway No. 50. Go on through Maysville and Garfield to the point where the accompanying photographs can be matched. They were taken while looking toward the west. From this point, backtrack for about a quarter of a mile to the empty houses standing just below the highway. At one time Arbourville extended on up to the point shown in the photographs but that portion of the town has been gone for a long time now. These few remaining structures are the only surviving remnants of old Arbourville.

Here was the principal street of Arbourville, looking west toward Monarch Pass

The "Ginger" Peaks still dominate the skyline above the site of Arbourville

3.

ARGENTINE

ON THE HIGH PEAKS that tower above the valley of Peru Creek, road builders of the 1860s, hacked out a passable excuse for a transmountain wagon road. First called Sanderson Pass, this rocky obstacle course topped the Continental Divide at the staggering elevation of 13,132 feet above sea level. In a historical sense, this record breaking altitude has never been equaled. To this day it remains the highest single crossing of the Continental Divide along the entire chain of the Rocky Mountains.

For more than a decade Sanderson Pass existed as a toll road, carrying wagon traffic and occasional stagecoaches from Georgetown up through the later site of Waldorf, over the top, and down into the Peru Creek country. Sometime in the 1870s, its name was changed to Snake River Pass, presumably because Peru Creek eventually comingles its waters with those of the Snake River, although the point at which this joining occurs is some six miles or so downstream. By this time there was a regular schedule of stagecoach runs that had been established and the fare from Denver was $12.75. When the East Argentine Mining District rose to a position of some promise, a final name change was imposed upon the high pass. From that time to the present, it has been known as Argentine Pass.

Within a few years of the time when the original cut of Sanderson Pass had topped its lofty ridge, a whole string of mining camps grew up along the course of Peru Creek. Out-

Argentine Pass, the highest Continental Divide crossing in America

*With Grays Peak in the background, the Pass now shows the results
of many rock slides and decades of disuse.*

standing, and among the earliest of these, was the town of Decatur which was started in 1868. Like so many before him, the founder of this community had migrated west to seek new horizons, a wider and deeper rut, and to escape a past that had become intolerable, for reasons best known to himself.

"Commodore" Stephen Decatur Bross had once been a respected professor at a fine school in Poughkeepsie, New York. Sometime in the 1840s he dropped from sight, leaving behind a wife and two children in New Jersey. During the gold rush of 1859, he arrived in Colorado. Prior to its statehood, he served in the Territorial Legislature under the name of Stephen Decatur. Meanwhile, a brother of the "Commodore" who had remained in the east began to manifest a like aptitude for politics and was elected Lt. Governor of Illinois.

Inevitably, as the commerce of the prairies grew heavier, reports began to filter back to the Illinois Governor of a man out in Colorado who called himself Decatur and who bore a strong physical resemblance to himself. Governor Bross immediately concluded that the long lost prodigal had been found and made arrangements for a journey west. When Governor Bross confronted the "Commodore" and identified him as his missing brother, Decatur vehemently denied the relationship, and continued to make additional public denials during the rest of his life. Privately, he once admitted the relationship to a close associate.

Everywhere the frontier went, men like Stephen Decatur Bross, often with a past that they hoped to conceal, came west and helped to write frontier history. In addition to founding this town at the foot of Argentine Pass, Decatur was also active in many other Colorado mining communities before he died and was subsequently buried at Rosita in the beautiful Wet Mountain Valley.

In the meantime, life at the town of Decatur went on. In the early years "Commodore" Decatur had been its moving spirit. But for all these developments, life in this community must have been rather confusing. As its official designation, the name of Decatur survived only until 1893. When the Sherman Silver Purchase Act was repealed, a slump resulted and the town nearly died. In the process, it lost its post office. However, precious metals other than silver were also found in the valley. Shortly after the decline, deposits of gold, copper, and lead were discovered. An impatient crowd of miners moved back and the town returned to life again, but not as Decatur.

Federal Postal regulations stipulate that when an abandoned post office is re-established, a new name must be found. Hence, Decatur became Rathbone until 1902. Then history repeated itself once more and when the town rose from its ashes for the second time, it took the name of the nearby pass. After 1902 it was known simply as Argentine. Since Summit County was one of Colorado's original divisions, there was never any change in that designation.

Several mines contributed to the rather variable fortunes of Decatur—Rathbone—Argentine. Among them were such properties as the Revenue Tariff, Delaware, Peruvian, and the Queen of the West. At times they poured out a veritable torrent of riches. But often they could barely sustain a skeleton crew. By far the best producer of the entire valley was the great Pennsylvania Mine, discovered by J. M. Hall in 1879. Over the years, its production exceeded $3,000,000. At one point the Rothschild Company bought in and sank a 3,000-foot-long cross-cut tunnel. Since profits were good, the Pennsylvania Company erected a huge multi-level mill across the creek from the town.

During all of its life, Argentine was never a big place. Rarely would one find more than 100 persons living there at the same time, although one report exists where population was given as 1,000. In all probability, this latter figure really meant a total of all the miners along Peru Creek, not just at Argentine. Children from Argentine attended school at a convenient point down the river where a community school was built about halfway between Argentine and the neighboring town of Chihuahua. Several stores managed enough business to keep the wolf from the door at Argentine. One hotel, the Sautell, proved adequate for the town's limited needs.

The beginning of the decline of this town was a violent one. During the spring of 1898, when the annual accumulation of snow began to melt on Grays Peak, a loud crash split the stillness above the valley of Peru Creek. Sending a cloud of powdered snow hundreds of feet above it, a massive avalanche came pounding down the slope. As the air rushed in to fill the vacuum left by the snowslide a series of gunshot-like sounds split the silence around the site of Rathbone, as it was still known in 1898. Overhead, the surging wall of air echoed across the valley and boomed like thunder. An immense cataract of snow coursed and streamed around the fragile structures. As the avalanche gained momentum, power poles were uprooted, buildings were flattened by the inevitable concussion, and the single road was soon blocked. Gradually the violent uproar subsided and the awful silence that follows the "white death" settled over the valley. Except for the remains of a few buildings, the destruction of the village was complete. These surviving structures and a few new cabins came back to life briefly as Argentine. But after the town died the last of them were torn down in the early 1960s.

To see the site of Decatur—Rathbone—Argentine today, drive west over Loveland Pass to State Highway 294, which turns south from the western end of the pass. Gradually the road climbs upward as it parallels the south branch of the Snake River toward Montezuma. Before it enters Montezuma, the road turns sharply left, crosses a bridge, and bends to the right again. Just beyond the bridge, turn left on an unmarked dirt road. This is the entrance to the Peru Creek Valley. Follow this road for a few miles until the multi-

Collection of Mrs. Elizabeth Roller
This was the principal street of Argentine, founded by
"Commodore" Stephen Decatur (Bross).
Collection of Robert L. Brown
After the snowslide of 1898, the town was never rebuilt.
Argentine Pass crosses the background range.

leveled Pennsylvania Mill can be seen on the hillside across the creek to your right. At the point where a trail branches off across the creek to the Pennsylvania Mill, was the site of Argentine. Most of its buildings were on the "uphill" side of the road. Some depressions and a few foundations may still be seen. Beyond this point the main road goes on to the abandoned workings of the Pennsylvania Mine and another branch goes up the original grade of Argentine Pass, and quickly becomes a Jeep road up to the places where rock slides from the talus slope above have made it impassable from this side. So, abruptly, with avalanches of snow and rock, ended the chronicle of Argentine and of its pass.

4.

ARLOA

IN THE BEGINNING days of our nation, approximately half of the present territory now occupied by the United States was covered by forests. From a vague point some 200 miles or so west of the Mississippi River, the eastern forest extended back all the way to the Atlantic seaboard. In Colorado and throughout most of the Rocky Mountains west, a high percentage of the country was covered with timber. Many early pioneers developed the attitude that since trees impede the progress of settlement, it was praiseworthy to cut and destroy them. However, there were many legitimate uses for lumber too, and therefore justifiable reasons for timbering operations. A desire to gain access to the magnificent stands of pine forest surrounding Lost Canyon was the primary objective in the founding of Arloa.

Since the Rio Grande Southern Railroad had already extended its tracks through this canyon between Mancos and Dolores, the future site of Arloa was recognized as a potentially good location in terms of ready access to both the heavy stands of timber and to the surrounding markets. Just prior to the turn of the present century the Montezuma Lumber Company began the manufacture of finished lumber at Arloa. The first sawmill was established there in 1900. J. H. Howard was president of the company and C. H. Mayo was the local manager.

Over the years, population statistics fluctuated rather sharply, and may reflect some inaccuracies. The first figure found showed 200 people there in 1900. Then in 1906 it had dropped to 25. For 1908 the figure rose to 125. By 1913 it was back up to 200 again. References in the Colorado Business Directory mention Arloa first in 1907. The last listing from this source occurred in the volume for 1914.

There were many demands for the lumber being cut at Arloa. Extensive mining and milling, railroad building, and the construction of new towns induced a demand for wood in large quantities. Huge boilers which supplied power for a variety of hoists and mills consumed many cords of wood annually. According to Ira Freeman, authority on the history of Montezuma County, much of the lumber from Arloa went into the construction of new homes in the growing city of Denver.

In addition to its sawmill, Arloa also had a small box factory and a planing mill. On the average, some 100,000 feet of lumber were cut daily. To move the felled timber from the forests to the town, teams of powerful draft horses hauled a fleet of heavy lumber wagons. Several crews of timbermen lived in the boardinghouse and took their meals in the company-owned cookhouse.

Beginning in 1906, Arloa had its own post office and B. F. Greene was the postmaster. W. W. Endner and H. Wagner served as postmasters in later years. In common with most other small settlements of this period, Arloa had a single general store, first opened in 1908. Prior to that time people shopped in Mancos, Dolores or Durango. Most of the materials for the Montezuma Lumber Company and some of the supplies for the lumbermen were brought in on the Rio Grande Southern Railroad. J. J. Evans was the station agent at Arloa. Two other names were also used for this town while it existed. In 1911 the railroad began calling the community Glencoe Station. Later it was known as Millwood.

Arloa's decline was directly attributable to a depletion of the single resource upon which the town depended. When most of the timber had been cut from the surrounding moun-

Arloa, the lumber camp near Dolores

Logging camp locomotives at Arloa

tains, the sawmill was moved away and the post office was closed down. At present the only reminder of life at Arloa is a huge mound of sawdust that marks the site. Alone among the towns in this book, Arloa is an exception to the author's preference for visiting a site before writing about it. The actual location is at a point 14 miles northeast of Cortez. In terms of today's roads it is between Dolores and Mancos, north of county road No. 184. When you have reached a point about 7 miles southeast of Dolores, Arloa should be below you, in the valley on the old railroad grade.

5.

ARROW

FOR MORE THAN 4 months, summer construction workers employed by the Denver, Northwestern and Pacific Railroad had been finding gold nuggets in the vicinity of 11,680-foot-high Rollins Pass. The year was 1903 and the tracks that would eventually go down into Middle Park had not yet been completed. During the autumn season of that year, when the aspen trees had turned to brilliant golden yellows, John Newman and W. H. "Bill" Wood rode their horses over the Continental Divide and proposed to make camp at a point part way down the western slope. As the day ended, the violent flame of the sun rolled back like sea waves across peaks, meadows and the far-scattered clumps of timber. Within a year the new town of Arrowhead would begin to grow at this same spot.

In the beginning, Arrowhead was conceived as an end-of-tracks railroad construction camp. With its abundant supply of timber, railroad officials decided that this would be a good location for a sawmill to supply ties for the advancing construction gangs. Tents had already begun to be put up as early as the spring of 1904. Permanent construction followed soon thereafter. Since it was located in a national forest, no liquor could be sold—legally that is. Quite apart from official regulations, a "private stock of booze" made this a fairly typical railroad construction town, even during its incubation period. Under the circumstances, an ample supply of hooch was considered to be of vital importance in this pre-railroad period.

After some initial slowness the last irons were laid and the tracks reached the new settlement during the winter of 1904. Scarcely less significant was the formal incorporation of the town, accomplished on December 29, 1904. With this act Arrowhead became the first incorporated town in Grand County. Shortly thereafter, the longer name was dropped in favor of just plain Arrow. An article in the *Denver-Republican* for September 29, 1905, stated that Arrow residents had more dollars per capita than people in any other town in Grand County, a not too surprising statement when considered in the light of the fact that it was the first and as yet one of the few towns to be established in that county. Incidentally, the population of Arrow in 1905 consisted of a mere 200 persons. Nevertheless, some 2,000 persons who worked in the vicinity received their mail at the newly established post office.

With the town's incorporation, Forest Service restrictions were waived and a veritable horde of booze jugglers went into business. At one time there were 16 saloons and each one paid a $500 license fee. Most of them were located on either Main or Spruce streets. Those saloons that were located at the top of the hill enjoyed a reputation for throwing out their bad customers. When this was done they were tossed out far enough so that they rolled down the hill into a large mud puddle. The enchantingly stewed customer was usually unable to climb back up the sloping grade. That puddle, incidentally, became the later site of a Fred Harvey House. Under these circumstances, police fines were able to take care of most of the town's expenses. The only pay of Marshal Danby came from his fees and fines. But his job also carried the dubious fringe benefit of free meals at the local saloons. Arrow's jail was a 10x16 structure, built of 2x4s.

Recreation was varied. One night a logger, now remembered only as "Blackie," got juiced up in one of the local gin mills and tried to lick all of the Swedes in the camp. The graveyard was northwest of the town. In winter, the local undertaker used a specially built sled to pull the corpses up to the cemetery. In this high and rarefied atmosphere, immune from raids by stewards of civic welfare, Arrow also developed a "honky tonk" district where both gambling and sporting houses were allowed to operate. For those residents with families, there was a community hall where dances and other social functions were held. One night several of the "girls" from the line crashed a family dance. Quickly, and with a great show of ostentation, they were put out. In common with many "wide open" towns where some of the baser human impulses were easily accommodated, women could walk the streets at night with comparative safety. Hardly anyone locked his door after dark. Arrow even had a Sunday School.

Although Arrow's streets were not graded, there were two street lights, at the corners of Aspen and Spruce streets and at Pine Street. These were turned on automatically at dusk each night. A free waterworks, owned by the community, brought running water to nearly all of the houses. In the beginning Arrow's homes were primarily log-type structures. All were innocent of plaster.

David Moffat's Denver Northwestern and Pacific was a pioneer attempt at building a line across the Rockies, thus connecting Denver with Salt Lake City. With the passage of time, this railroad became a major factor in the life of Arrow. Its route across Rollins Pass had long been used by Hahns Peak miners who were on the way to Denver, 75 miles away. After the railroad was established, Arrow became the western terminus for 1 day excursion trips out of Denver.

An early Colorado business directory listed the commercial enterprises at 9,584-foot-high Arrow. They included several restaurants, a general store, livery stable, boardinghouses and those 16 saloons. One of these establishments bore the unique name of Denver Railroad News and Hotel Company

Eating House. Another hostelry was Mrs. E. A. Linniger's Hotel and Rest. To provide competition, there was also the M. Wolfe saloon and Furnished Rooms Establishment. The A. H. Parker Hotel, the Chancey De Puy Hotel and Ed Mc-Donald's saloon were also listed.

Jack Graham's Restaurant was perhaps the most notable eating house at Arrow. Graham served 25¢ meals with no frills. Without benefit of a menu, customers could eat whatever was put before them or go hungry. No female help served the meals. Tin plates and cups and iron utensils were used to discourage theft. If you desired a drink with your meal, there was a barrel of water that stood by the door. The bellicose Graham was rather sensitive about the place and defied anyone to find fault. Once, so the story goes, a lady visitor refused to eat in the same room with men, and stayed outside. At one point she asked Jack Graham if the men inside were through discussing the meal. Graham replied that they were, "through, but still cussing it."

In addition to the railroad, lumbering was also an important facet in the economic life of Arrow. Shortly after the coming of the trains, this became an important shipping point for the many sawmills in the area. The Colorado Business Directory listed the Colonial Lumber Company and the Fraser River Lumber Company as being most prominent. Many sawmills came and went during the town's life. Among them, the rate of business failure seems to have been quite high. Some sawmills refused to operate on Sundays, and many of the lumbermen would work only for Republicans.

During most of its short life, Arrow's mayor was Bos Ross, who also acted as a justice of the peace. By 1906 the decline had set in and only 16 people showed up in a head count made during that year. The post office closed down and the last residents got their mail at Fraser.

A lush growth of timber now virtually obscures the site of Arrow, although the visitor may still enjoy a magnificent

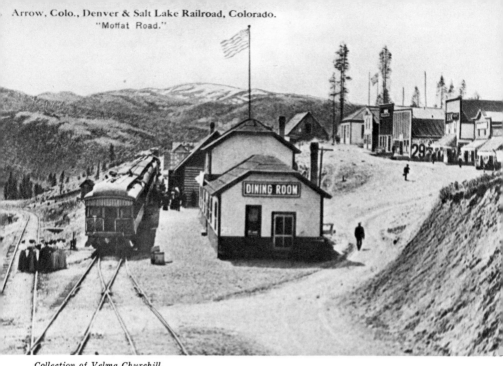

Arrow, Colo., Denver & Salt Lake Railroad, Colorado.
"Moffat Road."

DINING ROOM

Collection of Velma Churchill

In a happier day, here was Arrow

Collection of Robert L. Brown

Arrow in 1968

view of Middle Park. From a point near Winter Park near the West Portal of the Moffat Tunnel, a marked road with a graded surface will lead you to Arrow. The sign says Corona Pass. Actually this is Rollins Pass, Corona was the station on the top. In recent years the Forest Service has prepared self-guiding tours of the old railroad bed with numbered sites along the way. Arrow is one of these. If possible, get one of these maps before starting up.

From the eastern slope, a similar road goes up from Rollinsville on Colorado State Highway No. 119. Here a dirt road leads west to East Portal, eastern terminus of the Moffat Tunnel. There the old road starts up over Rollins Pass. Go on over the top and down the western side to Arrow. Although Rollins Pass is not high, it is located on the Continental Divide in a particularly exposed position. It is also narrow, rough in spots, and is not paved. When snows begin to fall, this is one of the first passes to be closed for the winter. In late June, it is one of the last to be opened up. These conditions should be borne in mind before attempting a visit to Arrow, particularly if you approach the pass from the eastern side. In good weather, this is a pleasant, very scenic and completely enjoyable trip.

Although this picture was labeled Rollins Pass, this view showed the earlier approach to the pass from above Apex.

With James Peak in the background, this once important thoroughfare is now a quiet back-country road.

6.

ASHCROFT

MEMORIES OF THE BLOODY Meeker Massacre were still fresh in pioneer minds during the winter of 1879-80 when T. E. Ashcraft slipped quietly into the depths of Ute Indian territory. Ashcraft crossed the Elk Mountains to the headwaters of Castle Creek. There, close to the foothills of the Elk Range, he laid out the small and quite illegal settlement of Highland. The site was close to the place where Conundrum Creek flows into Castle Creek, well within the boundaries of land that had been set aside for the use of the Utes.

When November snows began to fall, only two residents chose to weather it out. Castle Forks was the name given to the place where they dug in for the winter. All the rest of the residents went out over the range and reportedly spent the coldest months at Leadville. Nearby Aspen had not yet been founded.

Several months later, when the ice chunks started floating down Castle Creek and April breezes began blowing across the valley, most of the people returned, bringing an assortment of newcomers with them. Another townsite was laid out during the spring of 1880, just a short distance away, at the Castle Forks location where the two men from Highland had holed up in the deep snows. At first they called the place Chloride, then Castle Forks, and finally it became Ashcroft, changing just one vowel in the name of the original founder. Many prospectors, in their desire to search for precious metals in the valley, swarmed into Highland during the spring months. For a time, Highland flourished. Then, later in the summer of 1880, most of the silver seekers moved up the creek to Castle Forks and Highland died.

Ashcroft flourished from 1880 through 1883. By 1881 they already had their own school, and in November of that same year, telegraph lines had been laid out across Taylor Pass, through Taylor Park to connect up with Crested Butte. One of the periodic manifestations of any growing, bustling camp is a "nose count." In nearly all such cases the figures were given in round numbers. Ashcroft's high tide of population growth was reached in 1883, with a report that 1,000 people lived there. Nearby Aspen, just 12 miles away, was still in its infancy and was not regarded as being nearly as important as Ashcroft.

Outstanding among the accomplishments of which the early residents of Ashcroft could boast were not just one but two principal streets, Castle and Main. Notable among the structures lining these thoroughfares were general stores, saloons, a jail, and one newspaper, the *Ashcroft Herald*. John R. Nelson became the first postmaster when Ashcroft got its post office on August 28, 1880. Four hotels, the St. Cloud, Farrell, Riverside, and Fifth Avenue, provided sleeping space for bachelors and transients who found themselves living and working in this remote corner of Pitkin County.

Among the mines contributing to the prosperity of Ashcroft were the Emma, Aspen, Silver Islet, Dreadnaught, Worthington, Unicorn, Unexpected, Hidden Treasure, Pauline, Alpine, and the Empress. This latter property is reported to have produced ores as early as 1869, well before any organized attempts at colonization. H. A. W. Tabor had an interest in the nearby Montezuma group and was a partner with Joe W. Smith in the Tam O' Shanter, a silver property that was situated at an elevation of 13,572 feet.

In retrospect it would appear that Tabor put too much money into the Montezuma and Tam O'Shanter. Although these two properties produced about $20,000 per month in

1892, they were usually run at a loss. Tabor himself, since money was no object at this point in his life, built a fine home at Ashcroft. Panels for the living-room walls were covered with gold-encrusted paper. Whenever his young wife, Baby Doe, came to town, a 24-hour holiday was always declared, with free drinks at the saloons. If all this sounds a bit ridiculous, just remember that H. A. W. Tabor was the man who spent 12 million dollars in only 13 years. The late Gene Fowler once observed that Senator Tabor always had a "spattered look." Tabor, it seemed, always got fully dressed before shaving. As a result his coat was perpetually flecked with little gobs of shaving-cream lather.

By 1882, Ashcroft had stagecoach service from two directions. Actually there were three separate lines. Two of them came in over Taylor Pass while the other operated over Pearl Pass from Crested Butte. The Western Stage line started at St. Elmo and crossed both Tin Cup and Taylor passes on the way to Ashcroft. Historically speaking, Taylor was the earliest of these passes. In the beginning, wagons were disassembled near the top of the crossing and lowered, piece by piece, down over a 40-foot drop on the west side of the pass, 6 miles above Ashcroft. Taylor Pass, an 11,900-foot-high crossing of the Elk Mountains, dates from 1879. It was named for Jim Taylor, one of the earliest of the Gunnison County prospectors and one of those responsible for the beginnings of the town of Tin Cup.

The somewhat higher Pearl Pass route came up by way of Brush and East Brush creeks from Crested Butte before crossing the range at 12,715 feet. On the eastern slope, it followed Castle Creek to Ashcroft. Pearl Pass was opened on September 7, 1882. By 1885 it was a jack trail, carrying pack loads of coal from the Gunnison County mines.

By far the most important of the pioneer roads into this area was Hunters Pass, dating from November of 1881. When the first wagon attempted its 12,095-foot-high summit, the crossing consumed an entire month of difficulties.

This 19th century view of Ashcroft looks south along the upper street

This rutted trail was once the main road through Ashcroft

Hunters Pass crossed the Saguache Range along the Continental Divide. When the mining camp of Independence was prospering on its western approach, the pass was renamed. Of this group of passes, only Independence still survives in a usable condition. Both Pearl and Taylor passes are now Jeep roads.

Actually, more than any other factor, Independence Pass was responsible for the decline of Ashcroft which began to fade in 1883 as Aspen, at the western foot of the pass, started to grow. When the Denver and Rio Grande Railroad reached Aspen in 1887, there was no longer any reason to haul coal over Pearl Pass from Crested Butte. Entire houses were moved off their foundations at Ashcroft and dragged down the Castle Creek road to Aspen. Some mining continued at Ashcroft until 1893. There were still 150 people there in 1899, but by 1904 the total had dropped to an even 100. In a package real-estate deal, Ashcroft was sold to a New York syndicate in 1906.

In more recent times, the old town has been used as a movie set for a television series and there is a lodge operating in the vicinity at present. In winter sled dogs are trained in the valley to whisk visitors over the deep-packed snows. In summer, pack trips into the Elk Range often originate here.

Many of Ashcroft's old buildings still stand at this writing. To see them, drive one mile northwest out of Aspen on State Highway No. 82. Turn left on the road going toward Maroon Lake and abruptly left again on the dirt road that leads up Castle Creek to the south. Follow this road to Ashcroft.

7.

BALDWIN

IT WAS ALREADY after 5:00 p.m. and the sun was low in the sky when Jane and Louis Bass drove into our campsite near Almont and asked if we had ever been to Baldwin. Ordinarily we choose an earlier time of day for visiting a new town but the atmosphere was clear, the weather was warm and the destination was fairly close. Our route followed a good paved road, State Highway 135, that runs south from Crested Butte, through Almont to Gunnison.

At a point about four miles north of the latter city we turned northwest onto the paved but un-numbered Ohio Pass road. In the early days this was the principal route used by stagecoaches running between Irwin, Floresta, and Gunnison. Still later, in 1882, the Denver, South Park, and Pacific extended its rails up Ohio Creek from Gunnison. Beyond the point where the pavement ends, a good graded road continues on and forks near the site of the old town of Castleton. We took the left branch and continued on up the grade.

Off to the west the mountain vistas gradually become more rugged. West Elk Peak, 12,920-feet-high, dominates the jagged escarpment, creating a very beautiful and ever-changing backdrop for one of Colorado's prettiest valleys. Not far beyond the forks of the road, the old grade tops a small ridge and rounds a corner.

Suddenly, on the hillside above the highway, you get a first dramatic view of Baldwin. A rather large number of log-walled and dressed lumber homes still stand. As of May

1969, this town was one of the few unscavenged locations in the state. Great numbers of unbroken bottles still litter the ground around many of the cabins. Inside, mattresses still repose on beds, cook stoves stand in unused kitchens, pictures in frames adorn the walls, cook pans and utensils still hang, as if waiting for the people who will never return. With so much still to be seen in a completely depopulated town, the next step was to learn about Baldwin's history.

When the Denver, South Park, and Pacific pushed its steel through the mountains and up the valley in 1882-83, Baldwin had not yet been built at the present site. Grading crews grubbed out the aspen and sagebrush roots, scraped down the irregular mounds of earth, filled in the cuts and gullies, laid culverts, built up the grade and topped it with a ballast of crushed rocks. However, there was a Baldwin by 1884. It was the first name given to the later town of Castleton in the hope that Judge Baldwin, a railroad official, might be flattered into investing in the nearby mines. Later, in 1897, gold was found at the present townsite and a settlement called Citizen grew up there. Still later it was renamed Mt. Carbon before the Baldwin name was tried again. One other version of Baldwin's beginning mentions the earlier town of the same name as being located farther down the valley. It was moved, in this version, to accommodate the railroad when its lines came up the creek from Gunnison. Since the railroad archives show the tracks in place prior to construction of the town, the second story seems to be in error.

Baldwin's gold strike amounted to very little. It was coal that really caused the town to boom. The mine and much of its machinery may yet be seen in the gulch below the cabins, adjacent to the main road. In 1939, as the market for coal began to decline, the town began to die. Most of the families moved out in 1940. With the end of World War II, wrecking crews from the railroad entered the valley. By 1946 the last of the rails had been dismantled and hauled away.

Baldwin, the deserted homes above the Ohio Pass road

More of Baldwin's empty structures

Although Baldwin was already a ghost town, one nostalgic resident insisted on holding out to the bitter end. To Joseph Berta, Baldwin had been home for many years. Known affectionately to his many friends as "Peanuts," Berta became the self-styled mayor of his town. Each year he was reelected by a unanimous plurality of one vote. Until his death in 1967, Berta kept the vandals out of the old community. In accordance with his last wish, friends buried him at Baldwin. A new chain-link fence now protects his last resting place. Friends from the valley still place flowers beside the shiny new headstone.

At this writing, Baldwin is on private land and a barbed-wire fence has been erected to aid in its preservation. While the owner, a resident of the valley, has been cooperative about allowing interested persons to visit the town, he usually requests that nothing be disturbed and that you close his gate before leaving. Under no conditions should you trespass. Remember, a carelessly discarded cigarette or a thoughtless act of vandalism could remove this gem of a town from its hillside setting forever.

8.

BALFOUR

FROM THE STANDPOINT of chronological history, the record of Balfour can be traced all the way back to 1866. At that time the area had been prospected but almost nothing was done about developing it. Geographically, the town was located in a large, open meadow in the southern end of South Park. Both Currant Creek and Wilkerson passes provided easy access to the area.

Despite the early beginning, Balfour as a town did not get started until relatively late in Colorado's mining period. When small amounts of gold were found in November of 1893, it was inevitable that some overly optimistic persons would hail this as another Cripple Creek. All indications pointed to a glowing future, if you listened to the right people. In any case, some 800 persons were on the scene by the spring of 1894. Within a very short time, about 110 assorted log and frame buildings had been put up. One early photograph showing Balfour as a fairly large town carries the caption, "10 days old." If true, the town certainly grew up in a great hurry.

Within the business district were three hotels, the Crawford, which also had a restaurant, the Balfour and the Clarendon. Several stores, mostly general merchandise, and the Nugget saloon also occupied space in the town. One of the stores belonged to Tom Gill, who also operated the sawmill at Balfour. By December of 1896, a fourth class post office had been opened at Balfour. One newspaper, the *Balfour*

News Weekly, was published from November of 1893 through 1897. James Lightfoot and Joe Swan held down the offices of editor and publisher, and probably did all of the other jobs too.

In common with some other South Park localities, racial disputes arose among the miners. At King City, the Italians ganged up to exclude Chinese. Here at Balfour, both Italians and Chinese were victims of discrimination. Both groups were not only outlawed, but were prohibited from even entering the camp. Since the question of foreign-born laborers, who would work for very little, had become one of the burning issues of the 1880s and 90s, the attitude here at Balfour is not a particularly surprising one. During this era labor unions and agricultural interests banded together bringing pressure to bear upon the national congress. The long-range result has been a veritable jungle of immigration laws.

But for all these developments, Balfour lasted only 8 years. For more than 6 of these years, two daily stagecoaches maintained contact with the outside world over the two passes. Currant Creek Pass, northeast of the town, is a 9,300-foot-high crossing that dates from 1859. Essentially, it follows the path of a 60-mile-long Indian game trail that extended from the Arkansas Valley, just west of Canon City, to South Park. Wilkerson Pass, with its incredibly beautiful view from the top, also dates back to the earliest days of the Pikes Peak gold rush. Among others, H. A. W. Tabor and his family made their way into the mountains by this route.

Balfour died at about the turn of the century. Its location was 10 miles south of Hartsel, west of the road to Guffey, on the north bank of the buffalo slough. Colorado State Highway No. 9, which runs southwest from a point near Fairplay, will take you through Garo and past Hartsel to the desolate site.

Clark W. Fellows of Denver, who had a homestead near Guffey, once described for me how he had herded cattle in this area during the 1920s. One day he came to a spot where

This Carnahan photograph allegedly depicts Balfour when it was only ten days old

Here is the empty site of Balfour in rolling ranch country

great quantities of lumber were strewn about over several acres. This was the wreckage of Balfour. The hastily constructed buildings were unable to withstand the rigors of the severe South Park winters. With the decline of its mining fortunes Balfour disappeared quickly.

9.

BERWIND

IMPORTANT AS IT WAS in turn-of-the-century Colorado, coal mining is a short-lived enterprise at best. An underground seam of coal can be taken from the earth only once. With the passage of time, all coal deposits are destined for exhaustion. Unless some other economic basis is found, as it was at Walsenburg and Trinidad, even the most boisterous, prosperous coal camps eventually become ghost towns. Berwind was one of these less-fortunate locations.

Berwind is considerably older than most of Colorado's coal camps. It dates back to 1888 when the Colorado Coal and Iron Company opened up a mine there. A fine vein of coal, 6 feet wide, was found at the base of the mountain. It proved to be very good for steam power and for coking. Conditions were crude then. *Camp and Plant* magazine once published a picture showing several hovels at Berwind which housed 20 Italians and 500 goats. Later, in 1893, the Colorado Coal and Iron Company was consolidated with the Colorado Fuel and Iron Company and the mine at Berwind became C. F. & I. mine No. 3. David Muer was the first superintendent. He was later replaced by John Jennings who had been a mine superintendent in the coal fields of Pennsylvania. One new mine, operated by the Cedar Hill Coal and Coke Company, began operation in February of 1904.

Berwind's location was a rather fortunate one. Built at the bottom of Road Canyon, it was well protected from winter storms and men could work here the year around. A total of 393 men were employed there in October of 1901. On September 15, 1902, the Corwin school was opened. Since Berwind was small, the school was built at a point midway between it and the neighboring town of Tabasco. Bonds were voted by the two towns in 1901 and the school was erected on an elevated knoll that had once been a part of an old goat ranch. Berwind and Tabasco were just a mile apart.

For the Corwin school, Elsie Albert was the first teacher. She was later replaced by a Miss Armstrong. For many years the school was in session for ten-month terms. Generally speaking it was a day school with 60 pupils enrolled from both towns. A circulating library, for community use, was housed in the building. Late in 1902 construction was started on a new school facility to house a kindergarten and a night school. Among other subjects, there were classes in woodworking, weaving and a cooking class in which 58 men and women were enrolled.

Although Berwind and Tabasco shared a common school, they insisted on maintaining separate postal facilities. John Aiello owned the only general store in the town. Called Aiello and Company, it was housed in an impressive two-story building with an ornate false front, a large front porch and a genuine second floor European style balcony, a feature that delighted the predominantly Italian population of Berwind. Dr. A. L. Trout, company surgeon in residence, cared for community health and gave the usual health and sanitation lectures to the townspeople.

Berwind was located in the west-central part of Las Animas County, about 17 miles northwest of Trinidad on the Colorado and Southeastern Railroad. To see the site, drive south of Walsenburg on the old U.S. 85-87 highway or Interstate 25 to the Ludlow exit. Turn west here and drive about a mile west to the Ludlow monument. From there, follow the old railroad grade through Ludlow, under the railroad grade via a narrow tunnel, and up Road Canyon

Camp and Plant Magazine, from the collection of Richard A. Ronzio
Berwind, in the upper part of Road Canyon

Collection of Robert L. Brown
Berwind today is a mass of empty foundations

through the cattle pens at Tabasco. One mile farther on this same road you will find the ruins of Berwind, a tremendous town with gutted foundations extending along both sides of the road for more than a mile.

10.

BLACK HAWK

WHILE DOING RESEARCH for this chapter, one source was found which asserted that this town was named for Chief Black Hawk who tried to drive the white settlers out of the Mississippi Valley in 1832. Although this makes a more colorful story, it just isn't so. In actual fact, the town was named for one of the earliest quartz mills that was erected on the banks of North Clear Creek. The Black Hawk Quartz Mill Company of Rock Island, Illinois, was the manufacturer. One of their mills was freighted in and assembled at this spot on May 23, 1860. The town took its name from the big mill.

As time passed, the town went through a series of variations on the original theme. At one period it called itself Black Hawk Point. Then the "Point" was dropped and it became simply Black Hawk. On January 30, 1895, it became Blackhawk. Incidentally, this last change is still official although the more common Black Hawk has been accepted through practice. On March 11, 1864, it became an incorporated city by an act of the territorial legislature.

Black Hawk was never a mining town in the usual sense of the word. Instead, since most of the better-paying properties were situated on nearby Bates, Quartz, Bobtail, Gregory, or Mammoth Hills, Black Hawk became the milling and refining center for the whole district. At its peak, Black Hawk was known as the "Mill City of the Rockies." About sixty refineries were situated along this single two-mile-long stretch of North Clear Creek. Best known of all the mills at Black Hawk was the Boston and Colorado Smelting Works, built in 1867 on North Clear Creek at the lower end of town, by Professor Nathaniel P. Hill. Before Hill arrived, many ores had to be shipped to Swansea, Wales, for refinement. When he came to town, Black Hawk was in the process of becoming depopulated. Hill's smelter was so successful that Black Hawk acquired a second lease on life. In addition, there were thirty arrastras. When the employees wanted to live nearby, the population of the town rose to 2,000. Main Street, Gregory Street, and Chase Gulch were filled with homes and business houses.

A Presbyterian church, possibly the first such institution in the Pikes Peak country, was completed in September of 1863. The school next door dates from November 7, 1862. When the school was finally completed in 1869, it was considered a model for its time. It boasted two stories and measured forty by sixty feet. Black Hawk also had Colorado Territory's earliest cemetery, a burial plot was set aside in 1859 on Dory Hill. A. G. Rhodes, a transplant from New England, made Boston Crackers at his Black Hawk Cracker Works. In later years, he moved down the creek to Denver and operated a similar plant until he sold out to the National Biscuit Company.

Earliest of the town's newspapers was the *Rocky Mountain Gold Reporter*. Later, the *Colorado Miner* was published there. Still later, it became a daily and changed its name to the *Black Hawk Daily Journal*. Black Hawk had a skating rink in the 1870s. On week ends, dances were held for miners of the whole district. For the more serious-minded, lectures were held in Lawrence Hall. Quite a number of hostelries flourished during the boom years. Among them were the Pacific House, Sheridan Hotel, Mountain House, St. Charles Hotel, Colorado House, Four-Mile House, Clear Creek House, Tremont House, and the inevitable Black Hawk House, which was once owned by H. A. W. Tabor.

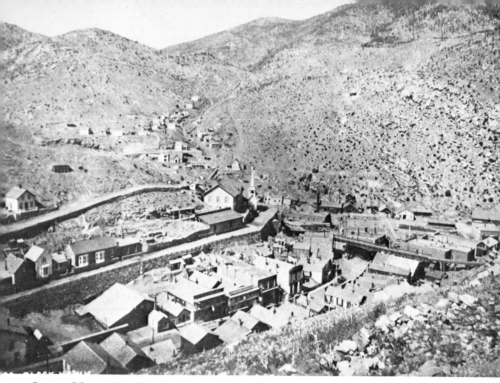

Here is downtown Black Hawk at the peak of its fame, with its principal structures stretched out along two gulches.

Many original Black Hawk landmarks were still visible in August of 1965

During the best years of the town, all sorts of businesses flourished at Black Hawk. Charles Leitzman kept a blacksmith shop. One forge and a wagon shop also did good business Five grocery stores, three meat markets, two drug stores, two banks, two theatres, four clothing stores and several saloons also existed. One cobbler made boots at Black Hawk for many years. Later, he went on to Gold Dirt (Perigo), where he made enough money from a mining claim to found his own business in Brockton, Massachusetts—the W. L. Douglas Shoe Company. He was later elected Lt. Governor of Massachusetts.

The story of transportation at Black Hawk ran the complete gamut from ox carts to a railroad. Probably the most interesting single aspect of this story involves the problems of getting the first railroad to Black Hawk (see Forks Creek). The Colorado Central Railroad began building in January of 1868. Some six hundred laborers were employed in laying the tracks and about 45,000 ties were required to get the job done. On December 15, 1872, the first train steamed into Black Hawk. For a railroad station, the town fathers provided a large abandoned stone mill. Holes were knocked out of both ends to allow the trains to pass right through. Although the railroad finally got to Black Hawk, some time elapsed before the connecting track to Central City was completed.

Although the distance up to Central is only a mile, there is a considerable difference of five hundred and forty feet in elevation between the two towns. Consequently, a two-mile-long switchback was erected at a cost of $65,000. The trestle spanned Gregory Street in Black Hawk, crossing above the level of the business district, in order to get above the creek. To gain more altitude, the main zig-zag was put on Bob Tail Hill. By May 21, 1878, the job had been completed. For many years there was daily service over this route. The last train to leave Black Hawk pulled out on May 4, 1941.

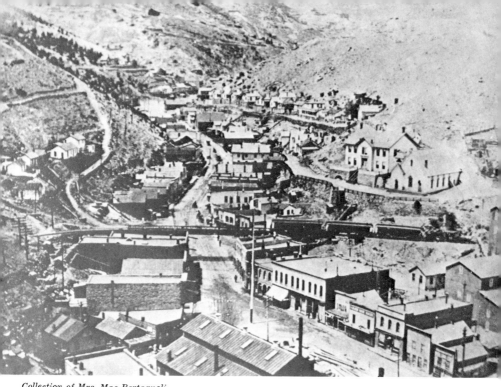

When the Colorado Central reached Black Hawk, its trestle was built over the top of Eureka Street.

Black Hawk, showing the original church, school, and many other buildings dating from the early days.

A second and most unique miniature railroad also served Black Hawk and connected it with Central City, Nevada-ville and Russell Gulch. This one was called the Gilpin Tram and its life span was a mere thirty years. It was built on a miniature scale with only a two-foot-wide gauge and was designed primarily as an answer to the high costs of hauling ores between the many mines of Gilpin County and the mills at Black Hawk. By 1887, it was in limited operation. As the years passed, spurs were built to many of the big mines while the tracks passed directly through many others. Within the limited mileage of its tracks, the Gilpin Tram gained a total elevation of 1,600 feet. Curiously, it never had a formal right-of-way. Regrettably, the Gilpin Tram met a most in-glorious end in 1917 when it was disposed of at a sheriff's sale.

Black Hawk also came in for a share of natural disasters. In the process of acquiring the lumber to build the several towns within the "Little Kingdom of Gilpin," most of the hillsides were pretty thoroughly stripped of their timber. During the spring run-off, nothing was left to hold the moisture. Consequently, being at the foot of the hill below these bare slopes, Black Hawk was flooded several times. The worst one came down on July 30, 1895. Finally, $32,000 was raised in the town to build a rock flume beneath the rather broad wooden sidewalk.

Black Hawk today is no ghost town in any sense of the word; but its fascinating history has roots that reach far back into Colorado's mining period. Between one hundred and fifty and two hundred people still live there and that number swells in summer. Despite pressures from Washington for a separation of Church and State, the old Presbyterian Church was converted to use as a gymnasium for the school next door. A very large number of the original buildings are still standing, in many cases seemingly cinched down to the steep slopes of the mountainside. It seems almost redundant to give instructions for reaching Black Hawk since it is situated on a busy, first-class highway. However, to be consistent with the other chapters in this book, here are the instructions. Drive west from Denver on U.S. Highway 6 through Golden. Follow this road up Clear Creek Canyon. At the forks of Clear Creek, turn right on State Highway 119 for seven miles to Black Hawk.

11.

BRECKENRIDGE

PRIOR TO THE ARRIVAL of prospecting parties which settled permanently in the valley of the Blue River, only one other group of white men is known to have been there. John C. Fremont, far-famed as "The Pathfinder" of our American West, led one of his five exploratory expeditions through this area in 1844. Fremont was an illegitimate child, but his illegitimacy was in the very finest tradition. His mother was a high-born member of the Virginia aristocracy, married off to an aged but wealthy planter. The father was an intinerant schoolteacher who was supposed to have been teaching her to speak French.

When Fremont himself picked a mate, he chose to elope with the fifteen-year-old daughter of Thomas Hart Benton, the most powerful man of his day in the United State's Senate. Shortly afterwards, the much coveted congressional financing for Fremont's westward expeditions became a reality. This proved once more that it's not so much what you know as whose fifteen-year-old daughter you marry. It was while on one of these explorations that Fremont and company traversed the valley of the Blue River.

In 1859, the year of the Pikes Peak gold rush, a party of southern adventurers who were in Colorado searching for gold, started out from Denver on August 2. Unlike most such pioneer groups, this one was not exclusively male. Its make-up consisted of 29 men and one woman. Although people from Georgia far outnumbered those from any other single point of origin, the group was actually led by ex-General George E. Spencer who had been a United States Senator from Alabama during the reconstruction period. For some unknown reason they bypassed Gilpin County and South Park, the two best-known diggings of that period. Instead, they traveled northward and entered the valley from across the range just south of the present town. While descending the mountainous slopes, a body of water was noted and named Silver Lake.

In the course of selecting a site, they finally settled down to mine in what is now known as Georgia Gulch. Nearby, there soon rose out of nothing a town of nearly a thousand inhabitants which they named Parkville. Most of the men started panning the stream at once. History records that the first pan of mineralized dirt to be washed in Summit County was valued at thirteen cents. The next was worth twenty-four. So jubilant were they at the possibilities of this discovery that most began staking out the ground into claims. Beyond this, little more was done that summer. The fact that gold existed in the Blue River had been established.

As with all booming camps, Parkville had its saloons, dance halls and a large theatre where early troops of traveling entertainers presented plays. One night during the performance, a burly actor appeared suddenly upon the stage. Following the customary statement of his love and grievances, he seized the innocent heroine and was about to carry her off when a broad-chested miner, who had been watching the play, strolled up to the footlights. The slightly tipsy pioneer leveled his revolver, exclaiming, "No you don't mister, you just drop that gal or I'll blow the top of your head off." Needless to say, the script was hastily revised and his orders were promptly obeyed.

Allegedly, only twenty-nine men and one woman (possibly the original group?), chose to weather it out during the winter of 1859. Since this territory, from a legal standpoint, still belonged to the Utes, their choice may not have been dictated entirely by the weather. Those who remained built a log fort just east of the campgrounds at the lower end of the present town. Two names for this structure have emerged. Some say it was called Fort Mary Bigelow, for the woman who stayed, while others refer to it as Fort Marbury.

From then on, most of the men spent their time sawing wood for new sluice boxes. Any surplus boards were saved for sale to incoming migrants who would arrive in the spring of 1860.

During its brief and reckless heyday, Parkville had served as the first seat of Summit County. As originally constituted, this took in a lot of territory. At that time the borders of this single county embraced everything in the northwestern corner of Colorado. With inactivity, many of the original Georgians became restless. In the spring they led a group of about a hundred incoming miners across Georgia Pass to the headwaters of the Swan River, a tributary of the Blue. Soon, the majority returned empty-handed, bearing bad news. The Utes, they said, were murdering settlers on the other side of the range. Widely feared for their hostility, the Utes were understandably upset by the encroachment of prospectors into their cherished domain.

The aforementioned arrival of spring brought with it a large influx of Argonauts, hoping to get rich quick before returning to their homes in the east. In the course of time, another large party of miners left Denver and the other surrounding low-altitude camps. Upon arriving, they began building cabins at a site about a half mile above the mouth of French Gulch.

By this time, the reputation of the camp had extended to most of the nearby settlements. Although the population was still mostly male, one source tells us that by the middle of June, 1860, there were already 8,000 people in the district. Most of the newcomers were distributed over French Gulch, Gold Run, Delaware, Iowa, Illinois, and Dry gulches. Some settled in Nigger Gulch, a name which was changed

Collection of Francis and Freda Rizzari
With Breckenridge in the valley below, a Denver, South Park,
and Pacific train pauses on Boreas Pass.

Collection of Robert L. Brown
From the same spot, here are Breckenridge and Boreas Pass today

to Barney Ford Gulch in a petition submitted by Senator Gordon Allott in 1964.

Out of this large nucleus of assorted camps, the town of Breckinridge was founded in 1860. The same Senator-General, George E. Spencer, now a one-year veteran of the territory, is usually listed as its organizer. Due to his avowed Southern propensities, he chose to name the town for Vice-President John C. Brackenridge, with the hope that this might influence the official to intercede and acquire a post office for them. Flattery worked its magic almost at once. Shortly after this petition was submitted, the post office was established. All of the new townsite was promptly surveyed and subdivided into building lots.

Later, of course, the rash haste evidenced in naming the community was regretted since Mr. Brackenridge had changed hats to play an active role for the Confederacy during the Civil War. Since he had already served their purposes, local consciences were cleansed by changing one letter to make the town Breckenridge from then on. Representative B. D. Williams, who represented the district in Congress, was a completely eclectic politician who concurred heartily in both decisions.

Although it is far less theatrical than the aforementioned story, a far more likely account of the naming of Breckenridge was recently unearthed by my good friend Forbes Parkhill. In the earliest editions of the *Summit County Journal,* an article stated quite simply that the town was named for Thomas E. Breckenridge (note contemporary spelling), a member of the original party. During the Civil War, Breckenridge served as a Major, returning to Colorado after hostilities had ceased. Curiously, he chose not to return to the town which bore his name. Instead, he settled in Durango where he lived to the ripe old age of 80 some years.

In the course of its booming economy, Breckenridge soon began to dispute the supremacy of Park City. Like most entrenched politicians, the "parties in power" at Park City guarded their prerogatives jealously. About 1862, a group of enterprising citizens of Breckenridge took the law into their own hands. A midnight requisition was effected, in the course of which the county records were stolen and furtively spirited away to be hidden in a log cabin. There they remained until the indignation of Park City had cooled somewhat. But regardless of right or wrong, at the proper time the records were "found" and new county offices were triumphantly set up at Breckenridge. This was a prize well worth coveting since at the time Summit County included all of the territory that is now covered by Grand, Routt, Rio Blanco and Eagle counties. In all this vast area, the only settlements were Breckenridge and its continuous series of satellite mining camps, located within a radius of eight miles.

No school district was formed until 1871 when the first educational facilities were established within a one-room log building at the corner of Carter Avenue and Main Street.

In most records, 1880 has been remembered as the year of the boom. At that time, population was still estimated at 8,000 for the entire county. Regrettably, Breckenridge, like most mining camps, became a wide open town with eighteen saloons. Three dance-hall type "honky tonks" ground out hurdy gurdy music around the clock and dispensed the usual varieties of "entertainment" and debauchery. One dance hall was on the site now occupied by the Fincher House. The other two were separated by a narrow passage between French Street and Lincoln Avenue. Later, these same buildings were occupied as a convent by the Sisters of the Benedictine Order.

Bridge Street was the principal business section, containing the largest hotel in town, the Grand Central. Most of Bridge Street was destroyed in the town's first fire. A later conflagration swept the upper part of Main Street in 1896. This was the most serious blaze in the history of Breckenridge. It swept both sides of Main Street between Washington and Adams avenues.

Most of the provisions for the miners were packed over the range from South Park by men on snowshoes. Later, pack trains of mules and donkeys were used. As soon as possible, barrels of whiskey were brought in and more saloons were opened. Traders wanted to value the gold at $16 an ounce, but the miners held a meeting to settle the question by refusing to take less than $18. Flour cost $42 a barrel. It was not a smooth white flour like we use today, but a gray Mexican mixture.

Saturday, the miners came into town for their mail. Most took back bread and pies, paid for in gold dust. Butter was $2.50 a pound, and eggs were $2.50 a dozen. Muslin was used in place of glass for most of the cabin windows, and a dirt floor was covered by many inches of sawdust, then burlap sacks were sewed together for a floor covering. Other rooms were paved with newspapers.

A railroad was built over Breckenridge Pass, running from Como to Keystone, in 1881. By 1883, it was completed to Breckenridge and to Leadville. A large joint celebration was held.

One of the outstanding happenings in the history of Breckenridge was the heavy snow of the winters of 1898 and 1899. The last train went out on February 5, 1899, not to return for 79 days. It had six engines pulling two coaches. Most stores had their shelves and store rooms full. Their goods, however, didn't last. Men had to snowshoe over Breckenridge Pass to get supplies. They would bring in as much as they could carry and one or two newspapers for perusal by the whole town.

Of all the men who snowshoed over the pass, only one was frozen to death. That year the snow came to the top of the Denver Hotel porch. To get to the street, people had to dig tunnels. The first train came back into Breckenridge on April 25, 1899. The whole town turned out to see it come in. All the church bells rang and the mine whistles blew to welcome it. The train actually arrived at 6:00 p.m. Fifty sacks of overdue mail were included in its cargo. Feed and grain had become a rarity for the last several months. During this period, beef had been the main diet of the people.

For most of its history, the growth and development of Breckenridge was closely tied to the production of gold and precious metals. Ever since 1860, large quantities of many metals, primarily gold, have been taken out. Among the earliest producing localities were the American and the Humbug mines. French Gulch and the incredible "wire patch" called Farncomb Hill contained the best of the mining areas. From Farncomb Hill came the largest nugget ever taken from the region. Affectionately named Tom's Baby, the formation weighed fourteen pounds. In 1901 Felix Leavick, for whom the town in the Horseshoe district near Fairplay was named, was in charge of the Jumbo Mill at Breckenridge. Something over one hundred men worked at the Jumbo and their bunkhouses were nearly always overcrowded. A reduction works was once built on the exact site of old Fort Bigelow. Today it is buried under a rock pile, left behind by the dredges. Frank Hall, in his *History of Colorado*, Volume 4, states that as late as the early 1890s, ruins of the fort were still visible.

Even though the entire Breckenridge country was platted for individual mines, the process of dredging accounted for a large part of the total production of minerals. Huge rafts, each equipped to separate the gold from dirt and rock, dug their own navigable channels across the countryside, processing the extracted elements as they went. Today's laws protect us from this wasteful and destructive process, but all around Breckenridge one may still see the huge, ugly boulder piles that remain as monuments to those who placed human greed ahead of sensible conservation practices and beautiful scenery. The dredging operations produced an income of about $20,000 per week. Although gold had been the primary metal for a long time, silver claims were found and exploited during the 1870s.

In addition to Breckenridge Pass and its railroad route, some other notable mountain crossings also provided access to the district. These included the difficult and currently almost impassable Georgia Pass, French Pass, lofty Argentine Pass, over 13,000 feet high, Webster Pass which crossed from above Montezuma to Handcart Gulch and, of course, the original Hoosier Pass which had been completed in 1860.

For many years, Indians were frequently seen during the summer as they migrated to and from South and Middle parks. Actually, their original hunting trail had led directly through the town. Fortunately, they rarely bothered the settlers. Although the land had originally belonged to the Utes, possession by the whites constituted nine points of the law. Legally, the Breckenridge country did not come into possession of the United States until 1866.

A great deal of controversy arose as to whether this land was actually a part of the United States. It seems to have been a part of the Louisiana Purchase, but western boundaries of this pig-in-a-poke land deal were only vaguely alluded to by Napoleon. Despite the rather free-handed way in which Colorado Territory was divided up into its original seventeen counties, a part of it seems to have been overlooked.

This resulted in the possible stretch of a "no man's land," as far as its legal title was concerned. The matter came to the attention of the Woman's Club of Breckenridge, which decided that something should be done. First attempts by the ladies to get the difficulty straightened out met with gloriously facetious replies from lesser officials.

About 1932, an employee of the United States land office, decided that some doubt actually existed as to whether a specific strip of land, approximately ninety miles long and thirty miles wide, including Breckenridge and a large part of Summit County, was legally a part of the United States. Investigation disclosed that a discrepancy apparently existed between the various disputed boundaries of the Louisiana Purchase.

Courtesy Library, State Historical Society of Colorado
Breckenridge in its days as a gold-mining town

Collection of Robert L. Brown
This particular thoroughfare is no longer the principal street of
Breckenridge. Inset shows trade token from S and J Saloon.

Finally, after much water had passed over the dam, the Woman's Club secured the aid of Congressman Edward T. Taylor. Through his efforts, the facts were formally presented to the United States Attorney General. After prolonged investigation of his office, it was ruled that such a condition could in fact exist. In order to settle the question once and for all, he suggested that Congress should formally annex the territory.

Necessary legislation was enacted and an elaborate ceremony was held at Breckenridge on August 8, 1936. Governor Edwin C. Johnson came up from Denver to preside. The United States flag was unfurled (officially of course), and the disputed territory was formally proclaimed to be a part of the Union.

12.

CACHE CREEK

IF CONTEMPORARY RECORDS and estimates were at all correct, Cache Creek was one of Colorado's very earliest settlements. Frank Hall, in his 4 volume *History of Colorado*, states that the Cache Creek placers were discovered and opened in the spring of 1860. Before landing in California Gulch, H. A. W. Tabor stopped for a time at Cache Creek. Here the future silver baron took some initiatory lessons in the labors and uncertainties of mining. S. B. Kellogg was another early Cache Creek miner who later achieved a degree of prominence elsewhere. Kellogg aided in financing and outfitting Captain Charles Baker's expedition to the San Juans. Later, Kellogg personally became a member of an expedition into these same mountains.

The ancient placer mining town of Cache Creek was located on a high plateau, above the west side of the Arkansas River and west of the town of Granite. Although its most productive days were from 1863 through 1865, the gulch continued to be worked during almost every summer until well into the present century. It was always a lively camp, comprised of about 200 people who had built log cabins along the gulch and up on the side of the hill. Cache Creek was incorporated as a town on January 10, 1866.

A good grade of gold was still being placered out in 1872 when about ten cabins were occupied. The Cache Creek mining company started up its operation in the spring of '72 as soon as weather would permit. During that year the entire gulch was owned by just this one company. Walter Jones superintended a force of 16 men. Their gross receipts averaged an ounce of gold per 10-hour work day per man. When possible, the mine was operated around the clock with alternating shifts of day and night workers. By June 1, 1885 these extensive placer beds were being managed by a Colonel Hawey, the new superintendent of the Twin Lakes Hydraulic Gold Mining Syndicate. About 60 men were employed.

Throughout its history Cache Creek was troubled with water problems. To solve this problem once and for all, a tunnel and flume were constructed in 1884. The tunnel was driven into the land that separates Clear Creek from Cache Creek. From Leadville, T. F. Van Wagener came down to boss the laborers at work on the tunnel. By March of 1884 some 1,400 feet had been finished. The shaft was completed from the surface to the tunnel level with hoisting equipment and headings running each way to meet those being driven from the north and south ends.

Three shifts of men worked on each heading, cutting an average of 12 feet each day. Their objective was to bring water into Cache Creek along land belonging to the syndicate. In all, the flume and tunnel cost in excess of $40,000 and was completed in 1884. The added water nearly tripled the placer gold output from Cache Creek. Fifty men were constantly at work from May to November. Most of the flumes and sluices on the old workings were renewed. For the calendar year 1884 the gold output was nearly $100,000. Frank Hall described Cache Creek as, "One of the best placers in the mountains, worked almost continuously for more than 30 years and still not exhausted."

Transportation was of great importance in that pre-railroad era. In the beginning most supplies were packed on mules or horses up the Arkansas and into Cache Creek. When the trail along the east side of the river was widened the pack mules were replaced by wagons. The toll road to Leadville followed this same grade in later years. Finally, long after

The early placer camp at Cache Creek

The site of Cache Creek is vacant now, except for the cemetery

the decline of Cache Creek, the Denver and Rio Grande Railroad won its Royal Gorge War and extended its tracks up through the upper Arkansas Valley to Leadville. Travelers destined for Cache Creek left the trail or the road at Granite and made local arrangements there for the last few miles to the placer diggings. The decline of Cache Creek was due to nothing more complicated than the final ultimate exhaustion of the placer gravels.

At present Cache Creek has no resident population. To see it, take U.S. Highway No. 24 North from Buena Vista or south from Leadville to Granite. On the paved highway, across the Arkansas River from Granite, look for the bridge that spans Cache Creek where it empties into the Arkansas River. Barely north of this bridge a dirt road contours up around the hill behind the white gasoline station. Follow this road up to the place where it levels out across a high, mountain-ringed meadow. Here the road forks. Take the left turn onto a less desirable road which will take you to the quaint old Cache Creek cemetery. The town was below you in the arroyo. Follow the steep road on down, keeping left at the next fork, until the road intersects with a rutted wagon road that parallels the creek. Directly in front of you are the huge gravel piles left behind by decades of placering. On the hillside directly above and south of the gravel piles, the remains of the original flume are still visible contouring around the hill. Behind you, on the slope below the cemetery, are the many foundations of the homes that once constituted the old town of Cache Creek.

13.

CAMEO

AMONG ALL OF THE mining towns included in this book, Cameo is one of the very easiest to find. In fact, a modern four-lane highway passes within sight of it. But it has not always been this way. Cameo emerged as a coal producer rather later than most of the other western slope settlements and its life span continued until the present decade.

For a long time men had known that the high and beautiful cliffs above the Colorado River contained rich deposits of coal. But so long as coal was available for the railroads and for the mills of industry at a reasonable price from Crested Butte, Floresta, and other locations in nearby Gunnison County, nothing was done about it. It was not until 1907 that these rich coal veins were exploited.

After many years of dreaming about it—but less than six months of actual exploration, John McNeil of nearby Grand Junction opened up the Cameo Coal Mine. McNeil was president of the Grand Junction Fuel and Mining company, an important western slope supplier. It was the exquisitely carved cliffs that gave the mine, and later the town, its unusual name. When viewed from the town, one of the formations resembled a head carved from the red sandstone, a Cameo-like stone profile that overlooked the valley.

Inevitably, the workers employed at the Cameo property began to despair of the four-mile trip from Palisade or the 15-mile jaunt from Grand Junction. As time passed, more and more of the men chose to move their families out to the flat area just north of the river. Here the little town grew up. Paralleling the river, the Denver and Rio Grande Railroad's tracks provided easy passenger and freight service.

Cameo's peak population occurred when some 200 people were in residence there during the 1930s. Several business enterprises flourished. There were the McNeil Coal Company and the rival Grand Junction Fuel and Mining Company. W. M. Kerr operated the town's only barber shop. W. J. Lee had an unusual occupation for a mining town, he ran a poultry business.

By far the largest commercial enterprise in town was the Rush Mercantile Company, a general store. C. E. Rush, the owner, was also the town postmaster. Combining postal facilities with the leading business was and still is a common practice in small settlements. For recreation, miners could relax in the billiard parlor of N. Vesakis. Cameo also had a school, a small white-towered frame structure that nestled against the hill at the northern side of the town. At this writing it is still standing. Cameo never had a bank, all such transactions were carried on at Palisade.

In 1937, there were still about 200 persons living in the area. That same year saw a curious fire which had the effect of isolating the town. At the southern edge of the community a narrow wooden bridge spans the Colorado River, connecting Cameo with the principal east-west highway to Grand Junction. Somehow a fire started in the middle of the bridge, burning toward both ends until the destruction was complete and the town was marooned.

After World War II, with the declining demand for coal, operations here began to shut down and the miners drifted away. A few still live around Palisade. At present there is a power plant operating on the Cameo side of the Colorado River, but the town itself is disappearing. The wooden bridge, as narrow as the original one, still provides single lane access to the site. Through disuse, many of the nails have

Contemporary Cameo, north of Interstate 70

The townsite of Cameo, showing school at right

begun to back their way up out of the old wooden planks, so watch your tires when you drive across.

At the northern edge of town near the remaining houses, a steel cable now bars access to the road that leads up to the mine itself. At this writing the Rush Mercantile building still stands, but its faded sign now proclaims the Cameo Mercantile Company, a later owner. Its white stuccoed exterior is chipping and many of its windows are gone.

Cameo's altitude is 4,774 feet, rather low as such towns go. To get there, drive 15 miles northeast from Grand Junction on Interstate 70 past the Palisade exit. At this writing the Cameo exit is still labeled and the ruins of the town are visible across the river.

14.

CAMP TALCOTT

COLONEL WESLEY BRAINARD left his home at Evanston, Illinois, in the 1870s and joined the throngs who migrated to Colorado during the silver excitement. For more than two decades he sought precious metals in Lefthand Canyon. In the course of his explorations he carefully prospected the valley from one end to the other. Scarcely less significant were his several expeditions into the side canyons that contribute to the main gorge. But the discovery that would justify it all eluded him until the late 1890s.

Early one morning Brainard brought his mule down to a walk in the dappled sun-and-shadow of the evergreen woods that line both sides of Lefthand Creek. Near an old landmark called Hanging Rock he made his strike and a permanent camp. To assure development of the property he secured financial backing from a party of Chicago capitalists headed by Lyman J. Gage. Mr. Gage was a noted financier who had directed some of the greatest money movements in our history up to that time. Since he was a warm and personal friend of William McKinley, Gage became Secretary of the Treasury when Mark Hanna masterminded McKinley's elevation to the Presidency.

Gage loved Colorado and often chose Camp Talcott as a place to relax. When he arrived to visit his properties on October 18, 1899, he told a reporter for the *Denver Post* that he had great faith in this mine and had decided to continue backing its development for at least another year. Following President McKinley's assassination in 1901, Gage sought to recuperate from his loss and chose the seclusion of Camp Talcott. He had planned to stay for three weeks but the pressure of official Washington business stirred up by the dynamic Teddy Roosevelt, cut his schedule short.

From the beginning Gage had designated Colonel Brainard as his superintendent of his properties in Lefthand Canyon. On one of his Colorado junkets Secretary Gage held a conference in Denver with S. S. Dick, president and chief owner of the Colorado Northern Railway. Although the reference to this meeting was quite specific, it should be noted that the Colorado Northern lasted only from 1883 to 1884. While it was a Boulder County railroad, it did not build up Lefthand Canyon. The Colorado and North Western, 1897 to 1909, seems a more likely choice. It did build down from Gold Hill Station into Lefthand Canyon, keeping its tracks up on the hillside above Camp Talcott to avoid losing elevation on the run to Ward.

In any case, plans were discussed for extending tracks to the mine before shipments were started to the smelters. Unlike many of its contemporary towns, projections were made to develop the Camp Talcott Properties before any production or shipment of ores. Called the Brainard Mine, large quantities of ore were taken out. Surprisingly, almost no shipments of low-grade ore were ever made from this mine.

Secretary Gage spent roughly $700,000 in development work on his property. Some of the money went into drilling deep tunnels to crosscut the rich bodies of ore. With the improvements that were made on the surface structures, Camp Talcott became a complete little city. Among improvements was an electrical plant to generate power for lighting the offices, the mine, surface buildings and the residence of superintendent Brainard. Here at Camp Talcott, the power poles were all painted white. Throughout the town, arc lights were scattered here and there, making the night brilliant.

This was Camp Talcott, below Ward in Lefthand Canyon

Except for empty foundations, Camp Talcott is gone

Another surface improvement came to the town when an electric tramway was built to carry ores from the mine to the mill. It also carried supplies to the camp. On some occasions the workers also rode this conveyor. Secretary Gage himself rode it on at least two occasions. Gage was fascinated with the life of the miners and enjoyed playing the role. He often donned the attire of a miner and descended into the subterranean chambers. In 1899 another mine, the Giles, was opened at Camp Talcott. By tapping into the electrical system, power was secured for operating steam drills at the Giles.

By 1909 the Colorado and North Western had been taken over by the Denver, Boulder and Western Railroad. The route still followed the hill above Lefthand Canyon. The railroad proved to be the cheapest way for getting treated ores to market. Things went well at Camp Talcott for many years. The town declined as a consequence of the mining slump that depopulated hard-rock camps all over Boulder County. The railroad continued to run until 1919. The tracks were torn out later and sold for salvage.

The site of Camp Talcott is bisected by a paved highway now. The easiest way to find it is to take the dirt road from Ward down Lefthand Canyon toward Boulder. Shortly after you come to the pavement, watch the skyline for the mountains that appear in the two accompanying photographs. Both views were taken while looking toward the east or down the canyon.

15.

CARDINAL

DEEP IN THE MOUNTAINS of Boulder County, the town council at Caribou met in its monthly session to deliberate upon a most vexing local problem. The year was 1881 and social pressures had grown increasingly intense as more and more families came to settle in the formerly wild mining town of Caribou. Reluctantly, the uncomfortable councilmen faced their duty. Gamblers and loose women, it seems, had become somewhat more obvious and flamboyant of late, as they pursued their respective professions. In this era of Victorian morality, such openness was becoming too distressing for the more staid and conservative elements at Caribou. When the final vote was taken, virtue triumphed, and all "ladies of the evening" and their assorted consorts were expelled from further residence and sinful practice at Caribou.

In a state of highly incensed indignation, these racy and newly-dispossessed elements packed up their trappings and moved down the road to the first flat open meadow, just two miles below and east of Caribou. Here, at the old mining town of Cardinal, they took up residence anew. Despite some published reports to the contrary, these people did not found the original town of Cardinal. Some old-timers used to insist that, "Cardinal was conceived in sin and dedicated to the principle that all men were fair game." Although these new arrivals soon took over and nearly dominated the economic life of Cardinal, the town itself actually dates from 1870.

In the beginning, Cardinal (Cardinal City) was plotted by J. D. Peregrine in the valley of Coon or North Beaver Creek, at the site previously described. During much of its history, the road that paralleled the stream up this valley was referred to as the Coon Trail. It extended all the way from Nederland to Caribou. The original town plot called for adjacent but parallel streets, on both sides of the main road, which was called First Street. Over one block in each direction were North Second and South Second, etc. Intersecting with these numbered thoroughfares, five named streets ran across the townsite in the other direction. Their names were Gold, Silver, Fountain, Quartz and Foundit.

To the south of the road that presently bisects this high meadow, stood the business district. Here were the post office, an assortment of stores, several saloons, an assay office, mine office, a boardinghouse and some cabins. Homes for the residents of Cardinal were on the north side. Population statistics at Cardinal rose from 200 in 1872 to 1,500 souls who lived there between 1878 and 1883. Mail service for Cardinal came from two sources. There was a daily run up from Boulder while letters and packages via Central City came up 3 times weekly.

Transportation to or from Cardinal was rarely a problem. Considering the commodities for sale there, someone was always ready to help provide transportation, also for a price. Three times each week, W. L. Smith's stagecoaches came up Post Road No. 10, the Coon Trail. Leaving Boulder each Tuesday, Thursday and Saturday at 1:00 p.m., they arrived in Cardinal at 6:00 p.m., before continuing on up to Caribou. At 6:00 a.m. on Tuesday, Thursday and Saturday, returning stages left Caribou, arriving back at Boulder by 12:00 noon of that same day. Quite often, people from Caribou came down to Cardinal to celebrate. Sometimes they patronized their former neighbors, who now lived in shacks and cabins around the saloon. But the original Cardinal folded in the 1890s.

Collection of Jane and Louis Bass
Old Cardinal, high in the mountains of Boulder County

Collection of Robert L. Brown
Cardinal today is a silent and empty place

In later years, during the tungsten boom after 1904, the Eldora Branch of the Colorado and Northwestern Railroad laid its tracks up the valley from Nederland. Although the original intent was to reach Caribou, their tracks never went beyond Cardinal. By this time, Cardinal had moved on down the hill a bit farther. This new Cardinal was down the valley, below old Cardinal, and also below the Boulder County Mine. A frame construction station was built at the north end of a long, high trestle. In general, Cardinal was now sustained by the railroad, until the tracks were torn out in 1919. All things considered, the Boulder County Mine was quite a good producer. It was first located in 1870 by Sam Conger, discoverer of the original Caribou lode. At first, the Boulder County was thought to be on a vein that was an eastern extremity of the Caribou. Over the years, the Boulder County produced silver, gold, lead, copper and zinc. At the mine there was a compressor house, some machine shops, and a blacksmith shop. Other mines on the nearby hills included the Sovereign People, Mammoth, Alton, Trojan, Laramie and Spotted Jack.

All of old Cardinal is gone now, but some of the structures at new Cardinal now serve as fine summer homes. To see the site, drive north through Nederland on State Highway No. 160. At the north edge of town, beside the bridge, turn west on the 4 mile long dirt road to Caribou. Where the road makes a switchback among a small group of cabins and summer homes was the later site of Cardinal. The original railroad is now hidden by the aspen grove across the creek to your left. On up the hill another mile or so is the empty meadow where the first Cardinal wallowed in sin. If in doubt, go on to Caribou and come back for two miles to the original site of the Boulder County Mine and the first Cardinal, a town that certainly had one of the most unusual economic bases ever to flourish among the ghost towns of Colorado.

16.

CENTRAL CITY

CENTRAL CITY IS CERTAINLY not a ghost town according to any definition of my own. However, due to a long and very rich association with Colorado's mining period, most people today think first of Central City when historic mining communities are mentioned. Here, probably to a greater extent than in any other 19th century Colorado community, an effort has been made to preserve and retain some of the historic landmarks and reminders of the town's colorful past. My reason for including this well-known location here is the same that I had for putting in Idaho Springs: an unusual and previously unpublished photograph. This one, from a 3½x3½ inch glass plate, came to light at a Ft. Collins auction where it and some other things were bought for 50¢. It now reposes in the collection of Jane and Louis Bass of that city.

Central City's history has been written, worked over, and rewritten so many times that I shall only attempt to sketch some of its highlights here. Back in May of 1859, John H. Gregory of Georgia struck Colorado's first gold lode in the gulch that now bears his name. As a direct result of this and a spectacular series of subsequent discoveries, four towns grew up. Because it was closest to the center of the group, this one became Central City. The others were Black Hawk, Mountain City, and Nevadaville. The latter two became ghost towns while Black Hawk and Central still have small but permanent populations. Central's population hovered in the neighborhood of 5,000 people during its best years, although a few sources have doubled this figure. Certainly for the whole district, the latter figure may have been realistic during the years when this section of Gilpin County was known as "The Richest Square Mile on Earth." A reputed half-billion dollars, primarily in gold, has been taken from the rocky earth of Gilpin County.

Building a railroad from Denver up to 8,500 foot high Central City presented some unique problems. From Golden, the rails were laid east to Denver, then west through Clear Creek Canyon to its forks, and up the North Fork. Construction crews of Chinese laborers laid the rails and ties. Black Hawk cheered its first narrow gauge train from Denver, on December 15, 1872. By wagon road, Central City is only a mile from Black Hawk. To get there by rail was something else, since Central is about 500 feet higher than the lower town. A complex of 3.52 miles of loops and trestles did the job and the first Colorado Central locomotive puffed into town on May 21, 1878. This line remained in use until 1931. Its grades, still visible, can be hiked today.

In the early days Central City rivaled Denver and was once considered as the location of the State Capitol. The town got its first theatre in 1861. The famed Teller House, most notable of Central's hotels, was first opened in 1872. It was still operated by members of the Teller family until 1935. Henry M. Teller, who served a total of 29 years as a U.S. Senator from Colorado, was largely a product of Central City. His fortune came from mining and railroad interests. Jerome B. Chaffee, who served with Teller in the Senate, was another Central City man.

The list of other notable persons who were associated with this community in one way or another could become as lengthy as a Biblical roster of begats. Horace Greeley came west to see for himself and made an outdoor speech on a pine-knot torch illuminated hillside, packed with miners. Mark Twain once rode Billy Opdyke's fast but kidney-splitting

Collection of Jane and Louis Bass
From an old 3½"x3½" glass plate, Central City, looking down from the Virginia Canyon road.

Collection of Robert L. Brown
From the Russell Gulch road, here is busy Central City now

stagecoach to the town and later told tales of his harrowing ride. George Pullman operated as a loan shark in the town. Allegedly, his idea for the folding beds in his Pullman cars came from the wall-mounted collapsible bunks found in Gilpin County miners' cabins. U. S. Grant, while still a General, also rode the Opdyke omnibus on his first visit to Central. When he returned as President and took his much touted walk over the silver-bricked sidewalk from his coach to the Teller House, he had been able to ride the Colorado Central Railroad as far as Black Hawk. If one were also to include theatrical luminaries, this list would be virtually endless.

Fire, the nearly inevitable scourge of many mountain mining camps, nearly destroyed Central City in 1874. It seems to have started in the Oriental shantytown that once stood at the end of Spring Street. Before it was brought under control, most of the central business district had gone up in smoke and flame. In common with most of its contemporaries, many of Central City's structures were of tinder-dry wood construction. One of the buildings destroyed was the historic old Montana Theatre. A few masonry structures, like the Teller House, had 2-4 foot thick stone walls and survived the conflagration. When the community rose from its ashes, it was rebuilt with the native stone and brick structures that may currently be seen there.

Like so many culturally deprived 19th century settlements, Central City decided it needed an Opera House in order to attract more and better traveling theatrical troupes. As the result of an active public subscription campaign, the present Opera House was built in 1878. Before the mining collapse, many of the great show business names performed on its tiny stage. During the depths of the last great depression in 1932, it was re-opened. Today's Central City Festival continues to attract great names for its brief summer season.

In its present existence, Central City depends in large part upon the tourist trade in its many diverting forms. First of all there are the opera and play seasons. Curio shops, museums, restaurants, and small manufacturing enterprises also flourish in the town. Jeep tours are available to carry the visitor to a variety of historic and scenic locations nearby. Winter casts a hibernating slumber upon a part of Central City, but a small resident population has kept the town from joining the ranks of ghost towns. To see it, take U.S. Highway No. 6 west out of Denver to State Highway No. 119 at the forks of Clear Creek. Follow No. 119 to Black Hawk and turn at the sign in the center of town. The "Richest Square Mile on Earth" is just an additional mile up the hill.

17.

CREEDE

WHEN NICHOLAS C. CREEDE first saw the Willow Creek country it was a thickly-wooded valley, very narrow, with bolt-upright cliffs on either side. Coursing down it was a placid, trout-filled stream with mountain flowers and willows along its sides. Creede was the first white settler in this nearly vertical valley. For many years he had ranged over the hills and meadows of Colorado, searching for veins and deposits of minerals.

During the spring of 1890, while prospecting among the mountains above Wagon Wheel Gap with a partner named Smith, he chose to sit on a fair sized boulder while eating his lunch. Without giving the matter much thought, Creede chipped away at the surrounding rocks while he ate. Suddenly he spotted an unmistakable piece of blossom rock, a type of formation potentially rich in silver. By May, his digging had exposed a promising vein which he named the Holy Moses, presumably from the commonly-used exclamation in the miner's vocabulary. The site was on Mt. Campbell, now called Mt. Moses.

The 80 foot shaft that Creede put down revealed a large body of ore located between well defined walls. When results of the first assay became known the ores were judged to be worth upwards of $80 to the ton. Realizing that he had a bonanza, Creede sought financial backing from David Moffat at Denver. Moffat sent one of his men to make an examination of the Holy Moses and report back. When the preliminaries were over, Moffat had agreed to pay Creede $1,000 at once. He also took a bond and lease for an additional $64,000. His eventual backing amounted to $70,000. In addition, he associated himself with Capt. L. E. Campbell of the U.S. Army, at Fort Logan, and with Sylvester T. Smith, General Manager of the Denver and Rio Grande Railroad. Together, they formed the Holy Moses Mining Company.

Meanwhile, back in the valley, Creede had found a second vein which he called the Ethel. At once the corporation authorized active work to be started on the two claims. Being convinced that still more mines might be found in the vicinity, the three capitalists employed Nick Creede to continue prospecting. All expenses were to be borne by the trio, while Creede was to receive a 1/3 interest in any workable mines he might discover.

A second prospector, Charles Nelson of Denmark, also entered the area and began prospecting during the summer of 1890. Before the first snows fell, he had located the Solomon and Ridge mines. These he sold to Judge Thomas Bowen of Summitville. Bowen, an exSenator from Arkansas and Illinois, had found the Little Annie mine and had become a leading capitalist in the area. The first cabins in town were those erected by Creede and Nelson. Next came a cabin that was put together by Captain Campbell, superintendent of the Holy Moses, for his use as an office. News of these discoveries produced much excitement around the state. Throngs of legitimate prospectors and would-be argonauts joined the initial pioneers in this richly favored new district. The very fact that Moffat had seen fit to invest here was enough to guarantee its value.

Before long a settlement had grown up in the narrow winding canyon of Willow Creek. It was called Jimtown. Some people preferred to call it Gin Town in honor of the great quantities of that beverage being consumed in local "garbage chutes." Flimsy tents became the first saloons.

Rough boards laid across two packing boxes constituted a satisfactory bar. A few chairs completed the illusion. Local brewing recipes helped the imagination from that point. One of these started with a barrel of whiskey, added two plugs of tobacco, some alcohol and distilled water. This rot was dispensed at $1 a gulp. There were 30 saloons in town by early 1892.

Roughly 200 carpenters were at work during the daylight hours, frantically trying to keep up with the demand for housing. Although the canyon was so narrow that there was room for only one street, cabins and tents were built as far up the sides of the sheer rock as possible. In many instances the cliffs became the rear walls. Some people actually laid stout poles across the rushing creek and built their homes directly above the water. Editor Richard Harding Davis came to see for himself in 1892. He found "a city of fresh cardboard, with pine shanties seeming to trust for support to the rocky sides of the gulch in which they have squeezed themselves."

Many gambling houses and saloons were among the first structures to be erected. Rooming houses were often filled within an hour of their completion. In some instances reservations were made before the foundation had been laid. New log foundations could be seen in almost any direction. The Palace Hotel was put up so hastily that a suspended blanket across the front served as the only door for quite some time. Large numbers of Chinese were everywhere in the valley. As usual, they cheerfully worked at the most menial tasks, performing the work shunned by Anglo-Saxons. Chinese laundries did a land office business. One early visitor described the celestial as having "a washboard in one hand and a can of hop in the other." Many Irish immigrants, who had been brought west to build the railroads, also found their way to Creede. Despite the expulsion of the Utes from Colorado, some had drifted back and were likewise working around Creede.

Winter descended with considerable severity. All around the town, the high mountains were thickly covered with snow. Until the onset of warmer weather, little work beyond the building of cabins was done. Merchants from Denver, Alamosa, Del Norte and Pueblo moved into temporary quarters and displayed their wares for sale. Soon they had neighbors as other business people rushed in to capitalize on the excitement. In the streets, principally Creede Avenue, the mud and muck were knee deep. Large numbers of mules, horses, and ox teams inevitably added to the mess. Loads of fresh lumber, cargoes of undelivered merchandise, beer wagons and wagons full of household furnishings were everywhere. Crowds of people with no place to go wandered aimlessly and jostled each other familiarly.

Two significant name changes were effected by the second summer. First, the name of Jimtown was dropped in favor of Creede. Second, the Holy Moses mine became the Amethyst and a small unincorporated settlement grew up around it. Although the Holy Moses-Amethyst name change has been reliably reported in more than one reference, maps exist which show the two as separate properties, leaving a margin for doubt concerning the name change. In another version Creede is depicted as striking the Amethyst lode on a previously unclaimed tract next to the Last Chance claim. Several other satellite communities also sprang to life in the hills above the Rio Grande River and Willow Creek. Up the canyon was a small settlement called North Creede. On Bachelor mountain an unincorporated cluster of cabins adopted the name of Bachelor. Nearby were Weaver City, Creedmoor and South Creede. The latter was located near the junction of Willow Creek with the Rio Grande.

It seemed to many that civilization had arrived with the fourth estate when Cy Warman started the *Creede Chronicle.* Later on, Lute Johnson brought a second newspaper, *The Creede Candle,* to town. Warman carved out his own little niche in history by composing a moving, quite traditional

and highly descriptive bit of poetry about the status of life
in bustling Creede. Although the last chorus of his work has
been rather widely reproduced, no attempt to chronicle the
life of this town would be complete without these lines.
Here, in its entirety, is the Warman poem:

> Here's a land where men are equal—
> Of high or lowly birth—
> A land where men make millions
> Dug from the dreary earth
> Here the meek and mild-eyed burros
> On mineral mountains feed—
> It's all day, in the day-time
> And there is no night in Creede.
>
> The cliffs are solid silver—
> With wondrous wealth untold,
> And the beds of running rivers
> Are lined with the purest gold.
> While the world is filled with sorrow,
> And hearts must break and bleed,
> It's day all day, in the day-time
> And there is no night in Creede.

Actually, the town was widely known for its all-night
illumination. Big flares burned regularly from sundown to
morning.

Theodore Renninger found the Last Chance mine when he
picked up a stone to throw at his recalcitrant burro. At a
later time he sold a one-third interest in this property for
$65,000. Five million ounces of silver poured out of the King
Solomon mine during 1892 alone. Some quantities of gold
and zinc were also mined in the tunnels near Creede.

For those of the fair sex who were respectable, a Ladies
Social Club, a Creede Study Club and a Ladies Bicycle Club
flourished. On nice days, the members of the latter society
whipped up the miners into a frenzy by pedaling around on
the winding mining trails in voluminous flapping bloomers.
When one irate husband denounced this practice as "dis-

graceful," his wife changed to Turkish striped pantaloons. He promptly suggested that she pedal herself back to Illinois but she spoiled his fun and took the train instead.

A branch line of the Denver and Rio Grande Railroad was built up the Rio Grande Valley and had reached Creede by way of Wagon Wheel Gap in December of 1891. Between 200 and 300 people arrived on most trains during the boom years. Each return trip also hauled the ores out to the smelters.

The first church service in Jimtown was held in a saloon. Shortly afterwards the Congregationalists put up a tent for their services. When Easter came the traditional services were held in the morning. That same night the tent was rented out for a prize fight. Jefferson Randolph "Soapy" Smith, silver-tongued bunco artist of many frontier towns, opened and operated an appropriate business establishment at Creede where the gullible were relieved of their heavily-laden pocketsful of silver. When news of the Willow Creek bonanza reached Denver, Smith recruited a motley crew of local gamblers and confidence men to fleece Creede. Within months of his arrival he had become the virtual boss of the camp. His establishment was called the Orleans Club. With an open palm he appointed officials but he managed public affairs with an iron fist. He later exhibited this same genius for organization at Skagway, Alaska; until he fleeced one too many of the local "Hirams." A vigilante committee called on Soapy and he died at the hands of their "local uplift" society. At one time the incredible Bat Masterson operated a saloon and gambling house at Creede.

Bob Ford, alleged slayer of Jesse James, also showed up at Creede and opened a saloon. In June of 1892 Ford got into a wild altercation with a miner named Edmond O'Kelly. While there are several versions of the basis for their differences, it appears that Ford was accused of persecuting O'Kelly's parents. Other versions of the story tell how Ford was invited to leave town because of his drunken sprees.

Despite local resentment, he refused to go. In another account he was blamed for the fire of June, 1892, which nearly wiped out the town. Since Ford supposedly had shot poor Jesse in the back, some people felt that poetic justice had been done when O'Kelly also shot Ford in the same manner. "Soapy" Smith conned the crowd out of their notion that O'Kelly should be lynched. When waxing eloquently, Smith could fleece the eye teeth out of a brass monkey. A huge crowd gathered in the street and photographers had a field day selling pictures of the mob, "a few minutes after the killing."

On June 10 the sporting element turned out en-masse for the funeral. Most of the town's gamblers, bunco artists, prostitutes, and others of their kind, marched in the cortege that escorted Ford's body through the main street and up the hill to the cemetery. Although there were no flowers, there was plenty of wine and lots of champagne. After copious quantities had been consumed by the participants at the grave site, several appropriate songs were sung and a number of bottles were emptied over the pine box as Bob was lowered into the earth. Everyone felt that things had been done just as the victim would have wanted. Ed O'Kelly was paroled after serving a short term at the Canon City penitentiary. Later, at the request of his widow, Ford's body was shipped home for re-burial in Missouri. That same day, the thrifty local undertaker dumped the remains of a negro murderer into the opened grave.

Creede had two fires. In 1892 a blaze in one of the saloons got out of control and consumed most of the structures along a half mile of the business district. When a second conflagration engulfed the town one night in 1895, the Denver and Rio Grande engineer was the first to see it as he pulled into the town. His shrill whistle woke the sleeping residents in time to prevent total destruction. A third fire cut a swath across upper Creede in 1902. The business district was also hard hit by a flood that came roaring down the narrow can-

Creede, on Willow Creek, at the height of its fame

Creede is now a thriving summer resort

yon of Willow Creek in 1936. In fact, there have been several floods here since the town was established. Stringtown, another suburb, was completely wiped out by the flood of 1917.

As prosperity continued, a new county was organized with Creede as the county seat. Several tracts of territory were taken from Rio Grande, Hinsdale and Saguache counties and the new Mineral County was authorized by an act of the general assembly on March 27, 1893. From this date on, affairs started downhill. There had been 10,000 people in the valley during 1892. By the end of 1893 just 8,000 remained. From India, a prime customer, came word that their mints had stopped all coinage of silver. Here at home, President Cleveland instigated the repeal of the Sherman Silver Purchase Act and darkness finally descended on Creede; there was a night after all. To top it all off, the country was plunged into the depths of the panic of 1893.

U.S. Highway 160 heads west out of Del Norte. At South Fork, turn north on State Highway 149 through Wagon Wheel Gap to Creede. From there the same highway becomes a dirt road and goes on across the spectacular Slumgullion Pass to Lake City. From U.S. Highway 50, west of Gunnison, the other end of State Highway 149 goes south from Iola and approached Creede by a much longer but far more beautiful route.

Many families still reside at Creede. In recent years it has become a favorite resort center for hunters, fishermen and those who love the great out-of-doors. Modern Creede is a fine, progressive little municipality with roots that extend deep into the most interesting period of Colorado's colorful history.

18.

EASTONVILLE

ALTHOUGH EASTONVILLE IS NOW an all but deserted ghost town, mining as such played no significant role in its development or in its subsequent life. Rather, this was an agricultural town, fairly typical of the many such settlements that once dotted Colorado's prairies, east of the Rocky Mountains. It was situated in the northeastern portion of El Paso County, on the Arkansas divide, at an elevation of 7,219 feet above sea level. At one period in its brief history Eastonville called itself the Potato Capital of the World.

Historically speaking, Eastonville began in 1872. At that time it was known simply as Easton. There were about 50 families here by 1880. It was not until May of 1872 that Easton got its first post office, located in Weir's Sawmill for convenience. One other source conflicts with this information and dates the first post office as April 1, 1880. In point of time, the town survived at this location for slightly more than a decade.

When the Denver and New Orleans Railroad extended its tracks across El Paso County, Easton was faced with a vital decision. After some discussion, it was decided that the town should be moved to a point about 6 miles to the northeast, on the railroad line. This "relocate or perish" action was systematically carried out in 1883. Shortly after life had begun at the new place, unexpected developments resulted in a change of the town's name. Postal officials came along with a request for a new designation to avoid any further confusion with the town of Eaton in Weld County. On May 27, 1884, the old name was dropped in favor of Eastonville.

Now, with its more strategic location, population increases were noted. The high point seems to have been reached when about 300 people lived there.

The late Carl Mathews, well-informed Colorado Springs historian, spent his early years in this area. He recalls daily stops of 7 passenger trains, going in both directions, as a regular thing at the Eastonville depot. In later years, the Colorado and Southern Railroad came into possession of the line. In addition to the potato business, cattle, horses, and sheep were raised and there was some lumbering activity in the nearby Black Forest.

For many years there was a thriving business district at Eastonville. Three general stores, the Russell-Gates Mercantile Company, the Eastonville Mercantile Company, and the Foster Brothers General Merchandise store, all flourished. One meat market, three hotels, Dr. Skidmore's drug store, and a school made life easier for the residents. Inevitably, there were saloons in town too. Three churches, a Baptist, a Presbyterian, built in 1887, and an Episcopal, also exerted an influence. A bakery, a livery stable and a newspaper, the *Eastonville World*, also existed for a time. J. B. King was the paper's founder.

In general, the most prosperous period in the town's existence involved the first two decades of the present century. Because of a failure to adopt some of the more advanced agricultural methods, there was a drop in the quality of the potatoes raised here. During the 1930s people began to desert the town. The inevitable decline was hurried along when a 1935 flood washed out the Colorado and Southern Railroad's tracks. By the end of that year only 75 persons still resided at Eastonville. When railroad taxes no longer supported the finances of the town, the future was bleak indeed. After the post office was finally closed, mail for the remaining families had to be secured at Peyton.

Eastonville was once a thriving little metropolis

The nearly empty site of Eastonville today

Today, the site of Eastonville is nearly empty. Only the cemetery, the Presbyterian church, and some empty foundations are still there. To see what remains at this writing, follow Colorado State Highway No. 86 east out of Castle Rock. Turn south on Highway No. 217 at Kiowa, and go on through Elbert for 11 miles to Eastonville. An alternate route may be followed by taking U.S. Highway No. 24 east out of Colorado Springs. Beyond Falcon but before you reach Peyton, turn north onto Highway No. 217 to Eastonville.

19.

ELKO

SHORTLY AFTER THE DISCOVERY of precious metals by Truman Blancett at Gothic in 1879, prospectors from the several nearby communities began a systematic search of the high mountains and contributing stream beds that make up this portion of Gunnison County. One such prospecting party, composed of men from Crested Butte, made its way up the valley of the East River, through Gothic and on toward the top of the range where Scofield Pass crosses over near the headwaters of the Crystal River.

There, on the divide between Gunnison and Pitkin counties, about 5 miles from Gothic, promising silver deposits were found near the foot of Galena Mountain. Rock Creek offered a ready water supply for both mining operations and for the building of a town. Elko, the community, derived its name from the surrounding Elk Mountains. Its beginning dates from 1881. Expressed in its broadest terms, word of the new discovery soon reached the outside world. In some instances the facts were grossly exaggerated. With increased numbers of settlers the number of mines grew, broadening the economic base of the town. Among the still surviving names of the mineral properties around Elko were the Duke of Wellington, Pride of Cinnamon, Slim Jim, New York, Spar Chief, Hard Cash, Lucky Star, Homestake, and Fairview. Several of the mines were located up near the head of Silver Basin.

In size, Elko was never a large settlement. Even the most

generous population estimates rarely credit the place with having more than 150 or 200 people at any time. Elko had a general store, a saloon, and there was also a post office in the town* From Gothic or the Crystal Valley towns, mail and communications from the outside world were carried up by stagecoaches that operated over Scofield Pass. To supplement the family larder, elk, deer, sheep, and an abundance of trout were readily available among the nearby canyons, then as now.

Meanwhile, in far-away Washington the United States began to feel the pangs of one of its periodic economic depressions. Grover Cleveland, after four years out of office between his two terms, had been returned to the White House in 1893. As President, his attention was centered on the problems of eastern bankers and businessmen, not on the debt-ridden westerners. Cleveland took several unpopular steps to alleviate the effects of the depression and none of them included relief for the least fortunate groups of his countrymen. In Cleveland's view, his most urgent task was to halt the flow of gold from the treasury. As a first step he sought and secured repeal of the Sherman Silver Purchase Act of 1890, thereby angering western mining men who had been profiting handsomely under the existing law.

With repeal, hundreds of mining towns all over the west, towns like Elko, began to close down as people started the inevitable migration elsewhere. For several years the town lay dormant. Then on March 12, 1901, interest picked up again and miners started coming back into the basin. Elko was revived when a 3,000 foot tunnel was bored into Galena Mountain. Financing for the tunnel came from Illinois capitalists who also put up an additional $100,000 for the erection of a big mill. By June 1, of that year the mill was ready. But two factors combined almost from the beginning, to doom the revived prosperity of Elko! First of all there had

---

*D. McLeod was the postmaster at Elko in 1883.

Collection of Robert L. Brown
Only one cabin and two foundations, indicated by arrows
at left, now mark the site of Elko.

Collection of Robert L. Brown
And then there are days when it just doesn't pay to get up

been a lack of knowledge of the real nature of the ores, conditioned by and carried over from the earlier operators. Second, the distance between Elko and the nearest market connection was too great and transportation costs ate up far too many of the profits until, after a very brief period, Elko died again.

To see Elko today, follow the same route taken by those original pioneers from Crested Butte. Their trail, now a fairly passable back-country road, is still there. At times this road is better suited for Jeeps and local inquiry is advisable. From Crested Butte, drive north to Gothic, then up past Emerald Lake to Scofield Park. At the southern edge of the park and still on the Gothic side of the watershed, a road branches off to the west for a very short distance to the few log structures that are all that remain of Elko.

From Carbondale, south of Glenwood Springs, State Highway 133 leads south through the Crystal Valley, Marble, and Crystal City. During 1967 work was done to open up the road over Scofield Pass for conventional automobiles. Due to the condition of this terrain, local inquiries about this road should precede your driving beyond Crystal City. When open, this road makes a steep but spectacularly scenic approach to old Elko. If time and weather permit, you might consider the easier road from Crested Butte for your access, with the steeper but more scenic Crystal Valley as your exit from the Elko Basin, making a far more interesting round trip.

A third route, for 4-wheel drive only, can be taken from Crested Butte to the old town of Pittsburg. Then continue up over Paradise Pass, a part of which is on the grade of the Colorado Marble Company's attempt to build a railroad over Yule Pass to the marble quarries. Then cross over into Paradise Basin and Elko.

20.

EMPIRE

EMPIRE IS ONE OF Colorado's oldest towns, dating back to
1860. At that time two prospectors came over the hill from
Central City. For protection of claims, the Union Mining
District was set up during the early 1860s. The town's name,
however, was not always the same. During the early Territorial years, it was known variously as Valley City, Swansea,
and finally as Empire on March 1, 1878. J. A. Love, George
Bendle and J. A. Burdick actually took out the first charter for the town of Swansea. There was a smelter here at that
time. When it was abandoned Swansea nearly vanished.

By 1862 Empire City boasted a post office, one hotel, a
blacksmith shop, a country store, and about a half dozen
houses. One of the homes was built by Dr. Bard, who drove
the first wagon into town and decided to stay. Most accounts refer to him as one of the first residents. Nearby Bard
Creek now bears his name. One account asserts that Bard
built the first structure at Empire. In the main street, a
wooden well house covered a 100 foot deep community well
shaft.

During this early period, much creek mining was done
and several crude arrastras were known to have been in use
here. There were also stamp mills on the site prior to 1864.
All of these activities suffered a decline after 1866 due to
the increased activities going on over the hill at Georgetown.

Since Empire was in the process of development during
the Civil War, many nearby landmarks acquired patriotic

names. The Union Mining District has already been mentioned. There was also Union Pass, a low crossing of the ridge that separates Empire from Georgetown. Empire's elevation is 8,603 feet and the top of the pass is only 8,640 feet high. Sometimes called Empire Pass, this crossing was only two miles long. Its western side is now closed by rocks and debris. Local patriotism also accounted for the naming of the three peaks to the south of the town. These became Lincoln, Douglas and Columbia.

One additional pass made a major contribution to the existence of Empire. This was Berthoud Pass, originally an 11,313 foot high Ute Indian trail that was widened by Captain Edward L. Berthoud in 1861. Currently this route is used as a part of U.S. No. 40 and covers the 30 miles from Empire to Fraser.

By 1874 some 200 people had made their homes at Empire. Curiously, the town was not actually incorporated until 1882. Four prospectors from New York were responsible for the final name change. Their names were Merrill, Spinner, Musser and Nichols. While prospecting, they found a particularly valuable silver lode and called it the Empire, in honor of their home state. One other source credits D. C. Dailey and Company with finding the Empire lode on Silver Mountain. At this point it would be nearly impossible to state positively which of these accounts was correct. Postal authorities took note of the change on April 1, 1880, or in 1882. (Two different sources disagree on this date.) In any case, the Empire lode brought about the final designation of the town and of its postal facility.

Ultimately a railroad, the Colorado and Southern, found it profitable to extend its tracks almost to Empire. Taken as a whole, this railroad functioned for a much more extended period of time than many of its mountain contemporaries. Not until 1939 did the service stop. At that time the tracks up from Idaho Springs were torn out and the original station building was moved down the creek to become a house.

Courtesy Library, State Historical Society of Colorado
The original site of Empire was below the present town

Collection of Robert L. Brown
Empire now, looking toward Union Pass. Inset shows
trade token from the Empire City Mine.

Empire today is a delightful little mountain village, located on U.S. Highway No. 40 west of Idaho Springs and just a few miles to the west of the new Interstate Highway No. 70. The road to Union Pass turns off to the south from the intersection in the center of town and is shown in the accompanying photographs.

21.

GARLAND CITY

ORIGINALLY, COLORADO's San Luis Valley was settled by small farmers and persons interested in stock raising. Since the Ute Indians also had chosen to live here, some inevitable conflicts of interest developed. First came the ill-fated Fort Massachusetts, conceived in a remarkable burst of military genius and built so close to the bluffs that the hostiles merely climbed up onto the higher ground and shot over the top of the stockade walls into the interior of the fort. Next, in 1858, came the more practical Fort Garland, built in the open valley 6 miles to the south. Its name came from Colonel John Garland who commanded it in the early days. In all, it was used for a quarter of a century before abandonment.

During the 1870s, long after the Indian troubles had subsided, railroad construction gangs began working their way westward toward the San Luis Valley. At that time the Denver and Rio Grande line across La Veta Pass was the highest in the United States. At the crest, iron rails topped the Sangre de Cristo range at an altitude of 9,400 feet above sea level. On the western side, the grades followed a general route along Sangre de Cristo Creek. Here, in Costilla County, where the railroad line emerged from the mountains into the eastern edge of the San Luis Valley, a construction camp was built to house the D.&R.G. laborers who were building the Fort Garland Division.

In terms of long-range objectives, the railroad was on its way south to New Mexico, via one line, and to the San Juan

Mountains via Alamosa to the west. Construction crews were already at work on La Veta Pass by July of 1876. When the railroad town company established their needed terminus settlement, it was decided that it should be called Garland City, although the railroad station itself was called Mortimer. Incidentally, the actual distance from La Veta was 29 miles and from Fort Garland it was 6 miles east to Garland City. That 29 miles was the longest single stretch on the whole D.&R.G. at that time. Including the siding, three sets of tracks paralleled each other in the town.

Two different sources give quite different dates with regard to the actual time when the tracks really reached Garland City. The first, and probably most reliable, source gives the time as the summer of 1877, while the other says that the rails had not reached the town until June of 1878. In any case, the settlement was already a going concern by the time tracks and ties had reached its outskirts. Garland City housed the men who were working on the Alamosa branch during the winter of 1877-78. When Helen Hunt Jackson described her impressions of early Garland City it had many tents and 125 ramshackle houses that had been built in the incredibly short time of just 12 days.

In *Colorado's Century of Cities*, Jean and Don Griswold tell us that the settlement had 4 sawmills. One hostelry, called Perry's Hotel, boasted 5 bedrooms. In actuality, their facilities included 5 beds in a row, each separated from the others by sheets that hung down from the ceiling. Mexican peddlers from the south soon found a ready market for their fresh vegetables and other produce which could be hawked through the streets of Garland City. During the summer of 1878, the population reached its all-time high of 1,500 people. Good water was always a scarce commodity in the town. To fill this gap, an Irishman drove a horse-drawn water wagon through the streets each day.

There was no mining collapse to account for the death of Garland City. Its demise came about when the railroad

Garland City, just sixty days old, looking northeast

Garland City is now a silent and empty place

reached Alamosa. Since nearly all of the residents had been employed by the Denver and Rio Grande it made sense to move to a location that would be closer to their work. Alamosa had been founded earlier and already had an economic base that survived and sustained that town after the workers had moved on once more to the next in a succession of end-of-tracks towns. Garland City was already gone by the early 1880s. The site is an empty field today.

To see it, drive west out of Walsenburg or east from Fort Garland on U.S. Highway No. 160. From the east, drive over the new North La Veta pass and drop down the west side on the good paved road through Russell. Just a few miles before you reach Fort Garland, watch for the place where you can drop down over the embankment to the south. Directly below, you will see the paved grade of the original U.S. Highway No. 160 heading off between two hills in a generally southwest direction. At this writing the old road is in the process of breaking up and of being overgrown, but it is still visible and, with care, it can be driven. From the point where you first left the highway, drive about 1½ miles. Then look off to the south, across the fences and railroad tracks. Match up the mountain contours with the accompanying photographs. Here in the open meadow, at one time, was Garland City.

22.

GILMAN

IT SOON BECAME VIRTUALLY certain that the Leadville district would be unable effectively to accommodate all of those persons who came in search of its silver riches. One among those areas that was settled and subsequently developed by some of the overflow from the "Cloud City" was the Eagle Valley. Nearly all of the early prospectors who arrived, starting in 1879, sought both gold and silver. At the beginning, this beautiful mountain-walled valley was a part of Summit County. Later, of course, in 1883, it was transferred to the newly created Eagle County. Since mineral prospects were of a promising nature here, it was inevitable that a network of settlements would emerge along the Eagle River and upon the steep slopes of Battle Mountain, 10,956 feet high.

Within a few years there were places called Eagle City, Mitchell and Roudebush, all of which were names for the same location. A like combination of names emerged for the nebulous Astor City, later called both Coronado and Blaine. Bell's Camp became the now empty Cleveland. And then there were Taylor City, Cooper, and the largest of the lot, Red Cliff. Some, like the latter, succeeded abundantly while others have not survived in the present century.

High up on the slopes of Battle Mountain, at an elevation of some 9,000 feet, a settlement called Rock Creek emerged. In subsequent years it became respectively Battle Mountain, Clinton, and finally Gilman. Its last designation came in conjunction with the formal founding in 1886, but without regard for the fact that life had already gone on there for some years previously. Henry M. Gilman, a miner who represented eastern money, was the source of the town's name.

At various times this area was a part of both the Belden and the Battle Mountain Mining districts. Judge D. D. Belden discovered the great mine that later bore his name on May 5, 1879. An impatient crowd of early prospectors dug something in excess of 100 prospect holes and shallow mine shafts. Its production was principally silver. Later that same year the enormously rich Iron Mask Mine was located and developed by Joseph Burnell, a Leadville newspaper man. It too was a silver producer. At the Eagle Mine, both the shaft house and the mill are partly underground. Almost alone among the prominent mines around Gilman, the Ground Hog was a gold property.

From the town, the miners climbed up over a zigzag trail to their work at the mines. Far below both the town and its mines, a large mill stands beside the Eagle River. From above, the unrefined ores are brought down on aerial trams. Throughout most of its history, Gilman has been a company town. To keep life interesting, there was a dramatic club, and traveling theatrical troupes sometimes played there when space could be found. Among the several hotels, the Iron Mask was the leading hostelry. There were some boarding-houses too. Since Gilman was a family town, a school was built quite early in the town's life. Many stores of the usual varieties were also found here. And of course there were many private homes, cinched down tightly to the steep slopes of Battle Mountain, with one foundation often falling in line with the next rooftop. A weekly newspaper, the *Gilman Enterprise* kept track of goings on in the valley.

For more than a decade the early communities at this site were served by Kelly's Toll Road, which followed the same general terrain as the present U.S. Highway No. 24. Then in 1881 the Denver and Rio Grande Railroad laid tracks along the river. At the Gilman station ore and supplies for

Rio Grande Archives
      *George Beem, early-day photographer, took this picture of Gilman and
      the Denver and Rio Grande Railroad tracks far below it.*

Collection of Robert L. Brown
                Gilman now, still going strong

the town and mines were carried up by the tram from the railroad tracks. Passengers could reach the town by climbing a series of wooden stairs. Population statistics for Gilman vary almost to the point of incredulity. Two different sources insist that 2,000 people were here during the beginning years. Other sources vary from a more realistic 200 to 300 in 1899.

A severe fire destroyed about half of the town in 1899. Before the flames could be brought under control, most of the business houses had gone up in smoke. In addition, the school, the Iron Mask Hotel, some boardinghouses and many private homes were consumed.

At the present time Gilman is the property of the Empire Zinc Co. of New Jersey. The town houses both the staff and their employees. Mining production is still a part of the picture too. Considering gold, copper, zinc and silver, the production for 1950 was over $7,000,000. This figure rose to a little more than $12,000,000 the next year. For 1953, however, it was down in the neighborhood of $5,000,000.

North of present Leadville and Red Cliff, U.S. Highway No. 24 begins its climb up Battle Mountain. There, on its sharply inclined terrain, lies Gilman, one of the most unusually situated towns in America.

23.

GRANITE

SHORTLY AFTER THE MIDDLE of the nineteenth century, the upper Arkansas valley had become deeply involved with gold mining. Placer gold was found first in 1859 and again in both 1860 and 1861. Hall's *History of Colorado* describes these early locations on the Arkansas as Georgia Bar, two miles below the later site of Granite, and Kelly's Bar, an additional two miles below the Georgia site, farther down the river toward present Buena Vista. Just for the record, both of these locations were active prior to the enormously important but later discoveries of gold in California Gulch. Quite apart from the usually followed patterns, placer mining never gave way completely to lode mining, and remained an important source of revenue to the district as late as 1899.

Then, a few years later, good placers were found at Cache Creek, Hawkinsville, Low Pass, Lost Canyon and Derry. In general, these sites were at slightly higher elevations, being located up in the surrounding valleys cut by stream beds contributing to the Arkansas River. Cache Creek was west of the river and Low Pass and Hawkinsville were above its eastern bank. Incidentally, all of these locations were to the north of the site of Granite, toward present-day Leadville. So it was quite natural that a centrally located settlement should grow up to house the argonauts who had penetrated the central Rockies to work at these remote locations.

When Granite City was founded, it soon became the second community of any importance in Lake County. The

"City" was soon dropped for the simpler designation. Originally, the remote town of Dayton, northwest of Twin Lakes, was the county seat. Within a few years, the booming Granite had begun to flex its civic muscles. In 1868 it replaced Dayton and became the county seat. For many years, it was the only place of any importance along the stagecoach road that followed the river between Buena Vista and Leadville. Here, at an elevation of 8,934 feet, between 500 and 600 people came to live and work in the 1860s and 1870s. There were general stores, saloons, the Creston Hotel, a smelter that used the Robertson refining process, and two stamp mills. Frank Hall, in his *History of Colorado*, mentions not just two but several mills that were running on free gold quartz at Granite.

Actually, gold lodes, true fissures of the yellow metal imbedded in deposits of granite, were discovered as early as 1867, although one source prefers 1870. Thus in an incredibly short time, early accounts had recorded the presence of several thousand miners at Lost Canyon, Derry, and at the Cache Creek placers. According to Frank Hall, H. A. W. Tabor was one of the prospectors who was busily learning about mining techniques at Cache Creek.

Outstanding among the mines located in the Granite area were the Good Luck, O. K., Belle of Granite, Hawkinsville, Low Pass, where arrastras were once used, and the Yankee Blade, which shipped over a half million dollars of ore to the U.S. Mint. On the average, free milling ores produced about $45,000 per season during this period.

Then came the Leadville boom, and with it the push by the Denver and Rio Grande Railroad to extend its tracks up the Arkansas River to the Cloud City. In the process, Granite gained railroad connections. By 1880, the D.&R.G. had begun laying tracks up the river from Texas Creek to Malta, just south of Leadville. At Granite, a station or depot building was put up and the fare from Denver was $12.50. All went well until 1926 when there was a wreck in the can-

Granite, on the Arkansas River, from a photograph by H. H. Lake

Granite in 1966, between Leadville and Buena Vista

yon just below the town. Twenty people were killed as a consequence. The railroad, as is customary in such cases, changed the name of its station from Granite to Yale, for the nearby 14,202-foot-high peak in the Collegiate Range. The name of the town, however, was not changed.

When Lake County was subdivided in 1879, Granite became the seat of the newly formed Chaffee County for a time. Then, in 1880, it lost out to Buena Vista. When the silver boom really opened up around Leadville, particularly in California Gulch, Granite began to lose out as people moved up the valley to the richer diggings. At one point in the 1880s less than 100 persons still resided in the town. Hydraulic mining, however, was carried on here as late as 1911.

Back in the spring of 1874, when the town was still in its raw infancy, Granite was the scene of a rank example of western injustice. This happening was the very type of incident that contemporary script writers love to think of as having been typical of the 19th century American West. It all began as a legal fight over the use of and rights to water from the Browns Creek ditches which carried water down to the Arkansas from the west. One thing led to another until a rancher named George Harrington was shot and killed. When a heated dispute from the previous day was recalled, Harrington's neighbor, Elijah Gibbs, was arrested.

Since local feeling ran high, a change of venue to Denver was arranged. Gibbs went on trial, but there was no actual firsthand evidence that could be presented against him and he was subsequently acquitted. By autumn, he had returned to his ranch. Some dissatisfaction with the verdict soon became manifest at Granite and there was an attempt to arrest and lynch Gibbs. While the ensuing fight was going on, Elijah Gibbs killed three members of his would-be lynching party. In an attempt to restore order, a safety committee was organized and several persons were ordered out of the county.

During this period of Granite's existence, the county and probate judge was Elias F. Dyer, son of the famed Methodist circuit rider. Acting as a Justice of the Peace, Dyer issued warrants for the arrest of several members of the newly formed committee. When they appeared at Granite for trial, all were heavily armed. To further complicate matters, the sheriff was unable to make them surrender their weapons. The case was dismissed on the morning of July 3, 1875, and Judge Dyer was assassinated in his own courtroom. To make things still worse, little effort was ever made to arrest his assassins.

Currently the population of Granite consists of fifty people. The town itself is now a collection of weathered frame houses, still standing beside the river at the bottom of a ravine. To see it, simply drive south out of Leadville on U.S. Highway 24, past the turnoff to Twin Lakes and on to Granite. An alternate route may be followed by taking the same highway north out of Buena Vista.

24.

HAHNS PEAK

JOSEPH HAHN WAS A TOUGH, solitary mountain prospector. His worldly goods consisted of the clothes he wore, the horse between his knees and the gear carried in his packs. With two companions he had already crossed the Continental Divide and had come out of the foothills of the Park Range before dropping into the basking valley, tawny and warm, that lay below him. Farther west the Elkhead Mountains of northern Colorado began to cast their long, purple, late-afternoon shadows across the land. It was late summer, 1862.

Hahn and his friends walked their tired mounts, lounging in their saddles, while behind, their packhorses nodded at the end of a lead rope. Off to the northwest the jagged snow-capped peaks of Wyoming's Sierra Madre Mountains loomed tall against the darkening sky. Near the barren 10,824-foot-high undulation which men would later call Hahns Peak, they allowed their horses to rest while they built a fire and spread their bedrolls on the ground. Soon the coffeepot spouted steam from its spout as the men began to eat their evening meal. As darkness fell, the wind's raw breath carried a shivering mention of fall. Within two days of his arrival in this valley, Hahn had found placer gold.

Although the Hahn discovery is fairly well documented, differences of opinion do exist. Instead of the 1862 date some sources prefer 1865. The authoritative *History of Colorado* by Frank Hall does not even credit Hahn with the discovery. Hall states that a Captain Joseph or George Way started from

Empire and made the first discovery in 1864. Upon returning, Way told his story to Joseph Hahn, a German sawmill
employee at Empire. That next summer (1865) Way, Hahn,
and W. A. Doyle of Black Hawk went back to explore Way's
placers. Hall describes how he personally met and shared
lunch with these men on the top of Berthoud pass. Primacy
is not always easy to establish.

During the winter of 1865-66 (Hall says it was May),
Hahn led a party of 50 rugged individuals on dog sleds and
with pack animals through 4-6 feet of snow to the site of his
discovery. Except for a well-founded fear of the Ute Indians who guarded this valley jealously, Hahn's party would
have been larger. With breaths showing white in the still
cold, the Hahn-Way party examined the stark, snow-en-
crusted valley, sloping off to the south behind them. Here,
in early June, they laid out a town, erected log cabins, whip-
sawed lumber for sluices and settled in. For a name, they
chose Poverty Flats, sometimes called Poverty Bar. Joseph
Hahn was elected president of the mining district and the
nearby peak was named for him. On one occasion the Utes,
under Chief Colerow, came up to see what these crazy pale-
faces were doing. The miners gave them food and the Utes
left peaceably.

Just two miles away, a second town was started. In the
beginning it was called National City. As time passed, National City became the residence of the provincial owners
of the nearby mines, known to the workers as the "big Bugs."
As this derisive term grew acceptable through use, the name
of National City was changed to Bugtown. Here, no work
was permitted on the Sabbath and no drinking or gambling
establishments were allowed to dissipate the men's morals.
Abstinence and celibacy weighed heavily on the minds of the
bachelors of Bugtown.

Since Poverty Flats was always a wide open place, it became more popular with off-duty miners. When mining
went into its first slump, Bugtown vanished. Like its neigh-

bor, Poverty Flats also changed its name. Following the lead of the mining district and the already named mountain, Poverty Flats became Hahns Peak.

When early snows heralded the arrival of winter once more, most of the residents got out. Only Hahn, Doyle, and Way decided to spend the winter at their town. All went well for a time, until food supplies ran low. Way started out alone to get relief from Empire. He never returned. Some accounts speculate that he sold out his friends. Hahn and Doyle waited in their cabin until, in April, their food was almost gone. With almost no other choice left, the two men decided to snowshoe to Empire. When overtaken by a storm, they became lost and made a most difficult crossing of the Gore Range in Middle Park. Sleet swirled around them like a milkshake froth. Lowering clouds hugged the ground, blanketing the area in an eerie world of white. After much suffering, they reached the Muddy, a tributary of the Grand (now Colorado) River. Still lost, they wrapped themselves in blankets and settled in for the night.

Next morning Hahn was too weak to go on. Doyle went for help. It was a day of intermittent snow squalls and harsh, cold sunlight. Clouds, churned by the storm, boiled around the valley. He wandered all day, finding no food or people. When he retraced his steps to their camp that night, Hahn was already dead. Again the next day Doyle searched but without success. The following day, miraculously, he was found by two ranchers, named Sumner and Franklin, searching for strayed stock. When located Doyle was snowblind and "half crazy" from personal suffering. He was taken to the stock cabin of John S. Jones.

After hearing his story, a party went out to search for Hahn's body, estimated by Doyle to be 10-15 miles away. Due to an error in Doyle's calculations, the body was not found until the next November. The actual location was just a mile from the Jones cabin and a half mile up from the mouth of the Muddy River.

When summer came again, people began their annual return to Hahns Peak. Here, at an elevation of 8,200 feet, a
year-around community evolved. In winter, supplies and
mail were brought in on snowshoes. In summer, a horseback
"pony express" type of operation carried the mail in from
Steamboat Springs, 25 miles to the south. A stagecoach connection could be made with Rawlins, Wyoming, and the
fare was $15.00. To Dixon, Wyoming, the cost of a ticket
was $7.00. The closest railroad connection was 110 miles
away at Rawlins, where the Union Pacific maintained a station. In the 1881 edition of the *Grip-Sack Guide of Colorado*
George Crofutt gave the population of Hahns Peak as 150
people. In his somewhat rarer 1885 edition, a population of
500 was shown.

At Hahns Peak, the daily wage of a miner was $3.25. If
single, he paid $6.00 weekly for his board. Geologists feel
that the gold here came from an extinct volcanic cone. Aside
from placering activities carried on in the early days, most
of the gold was extracted by high-pressure hydraulic hoses
that washed away the banks of earth. Three mining companies were active here over the years. In the beginning it
was the International Mining Company, which mainly
worked the placers. Later the Hahns Peak and the Purdy
companies became active. The latter firm took out between
$10,000 and $12,000 in 1874 with 150 men employed. In
all $5,000,000 had been extracted by the end of the century,
counting all operations. For a time, between 1879 and 1912,
Hahns Peak was the seat of Routt County. When court was
in session, lawyers came up on snowshoes from Steamboat
Springs to try their cases.

The decline of Hahns Peak began in 1912. Its demise as a
mining camp was directly attributable to a combination of
extreme winters and the high cost of gold extraction. After
the mining slump the town continued as a ranching center.
It was once the site of a bitter range war between cattle and

sheep men. The last available population statistics show a summer only residency of 40 people today.

From Steamboat Springs, on U.S. Highway 40 in northern Colorado, drive straight north through Mud Creek Village and Clark. Hahns Peak is 7 miles to the north of Clark and 20 miles south of the Wyoming state line.

Hahns Peak in winter, during the mining boom

Today, Hahns Peak is a pleasant little resort town

25.

HAYWOOD HOT SPRINGS

SEVERAL TIMES EACH YEAR, throngs of swarthy, stockily-built Ute Indians gathered here from various parts of Colorado's western slope to enjoy the soothing effects of the mineral waters that flowed out of the mountains beside Chalk Creek. All accounts of the history of this region agree that these hot springs were well known to the Indians and that they were probably the first people to see and bathe in them.

Then in 1877, the first of a long line of owners took possession by virtue of a chance discovery. John L. Dyer, the beloved "Snowshoe Itinerant" maintained a variety of Methodist Congregations throughout the mountains. Early in the summer of 1877 Dyer was in the Chalk Creek Valley with a man recorded in Dyer's account only as "brother Gilland." Together they climbed a nearby high peak, probably Mt. Antero. Following a difficult climb, the two men chose another route for their descent. By coincidence, they reached the valley floor beside a hot spring which flowed into the icy creek. Testing the water, Dyer wrote in his journal that it was, "so hot it would almost boil an egg."

The tired climbers shed their clothing and took a relaxing bath where the "hot and cold water mingled for the right temperature." While sitting in the stream Dyer decided that the two currents did not really mix together at all but flowed side by side. "The hot did not quite blister," he wrote, "and the cold did not quite freeze."

Father Dyer, as he was known, liked the place and prompt-

This early view shows some of the oldest buildings, including a bath house, at Haywood Hot Springs.

Several modern structures now occupy the old Haywood site

ly located a quarter section for medicinal purposes. After filing a claim, he built a log house near the springs, probably the first structure to be erected here. Unfortunately the Methodist Conference decided to move Dyer from the Arkansas Valley. He was re-assigned in New Mexico. Even more unfortunate, his claim was never surveyed and under the laws of that era he could hold his claim only by personal possession. He left with the hope that no one would jump his claim. But an elderly physician from Georgia "appropriated" the hot spring. Later on, at considerable financial cost, Dyer got him off the land.

Down through the years the hot springs had a multiplicity of owners. Its name has been Hortense, Haywood, and has occasionally appeared as Heywood and as Hayword. The name of C. F. R. Hayward, a *Denver Times* newspaperman, appears on one of the early town plats. He may have been the source of the town's name. On July 13, 1882, he was present on the first train to pass through the nearby Alpine Tunnel. In more recent years the name of Mt. Princeton Hot Springs has been preferred for this location.

Probably the most notable structure even to be erected at the springs was the huge four-story Antero Hotel. Ground was broken for its foundations in the late 1870s. But progress was slow and the walls were not completed until 1891. When its doors were first opened to the public in 1917, contemporary descriptions in the public press were unusual to say the least. Two of its four completely different towers appeared on the corners above the mansard roof. One had a square top and another sported a flagpole. Inside there were 100 rooms. Its exterior was painted green and tan.

A bath house and pool were completed in 1918. Both a tennis court and a golf course were ready for the opening of the 1925 season. But a conflicting grazing permit soon canceled out the golf course and one guest filed a lawsuit when he could not play the game because of cattle on the greens.

Transportation facilities were enhanced when the Denver, South Park, and Pacific allegedly paid $3,000 for a right-of-way easement through the grounds in 1880. Later, the railroad located a wye and a water tank at Haywood.

George Crofutt's widely read *Grip-Sack Guide of Colorado* described Haywood Hot Springs in his 1884 edition. He listed a population of 50 and mentioned that the waters were, "said to be of great benefit for rheumatism and kindred diseases." A publicity blurb in the *Union Pacific Tourist* described it as "seething fountains charged with health."

The stock market crash of 1929 and the subsequent period of hard times caused the hotel to close its doors. For the next 13 years or so it was empty except for a caretaker. Then in 1945 it reopened briefly as a private school. By 1949 it was up for sale again and a family from Texas bought the hotel, had it razed and the parts moved to Texas. It has since been reerected on a site in that state.

The Haywood-Mt. Princeton Hot Springs location is easy to find. Drive south on U.S. 285 from Buena Vista to Nathrop. Turn west on the recently paved road for 4 miles to the springs. Currently the original naturally heated pool is open to the public for a small fee and one of the original bath houses still stands nearby. On what would appear to be the hotel foundation, a fine new structure of modern design has been erected. Up the hill, on the other side of the road, a battery of new duplex apartments can be seen. Beyond the pool the road forks with the old railroad grade going to the left and an original wagon road to the right. Farther up the valley, the two roads join up again, providing access to the ghost towns of St. Elmo, Romley and Hancock.

26.

HESSIE

DURING THE WINTER OF 1891-92, Captain J. H. Davis located a small silver claim in Boulder County and put up a cabin in the hollow at the foot of Chittenden Mountain. His location was just two miles west of Eldora, and barely east of the point where the north and south forks of Boulder Creek meet and commingle their waters. Although the Davis claim was not a particularly rich one, word filtered out and the story apparently gained something with each telling. Soon a small nucleus of population had grown up around the Davis camp. By the close of 1892, there were 12 cabins, a boardinghouse, 2 machinists, a Justice of the Peace, 2 stores, a school and one sawmill operated by Quigley and Company.

When Captain Davis brought his wife to the settlement, she quickly made herself indispensable by setting up a crude postal facility in the Davis cabin. Within a few months the arrangement was made official and Mrs. Davis became the first postmistress. At other times Captain Davis also served as postmaster. In gratitude the miners decided to name their little town in Mrs. Davis's honor. By this simple act the name of Hessie was added to the map of Colorado.

But the citizens of Hessie never "took leave of their census"; the town always remained small. The winter of 1901-02 was fairly typical with 80 people in residence. Any chance for growth was retarded by the physical limitations of its environment and by the presence of its larger neighbor, Eldora, just two miles away.

In 1920, several of Hessie's buildings were still there

Here are Hessie's remaining buildings

Southwest of Hessie, up near Lost Lake, were most of the mines that supported the town. A few others were located along Jasper Creek. But the greatest producer of all was the great 4th of July Mine, a silver property located by C. C. Alvord on May 21, 1875, many years before Hessie was in existence. The 4th of July was a timberline property near Arapaho Pass on the Continental Divide, an area that is still confettied with snow even in summer. By 1900 the silver veins were nearly exhausted and the mine had been written off as a poor producer and was closed down. Then copper was found and the Consolidated Copper Mining, Milling, and Smelting Company was formed to develop the property. In all, three million shares of stock were issued for sale at $1.00 each.

Hessie's only brush with notoriety occurred on June 13, 1914. There were only a dozen people living there at the time. Among them was Champ Smith, a 50-year-old, gray-haired bachelor who had lived alone at Eldora since 1897. It was Smith who drove the Caledonia Tunnel into Bryan Mountain, located about a half mile below the town. Other residents involved in the case were Mr. and Mrs. Wilson Davis, the two Smalley brothers and their families. Mr. Davis and the Smalleys were also miners.

When G. W. Orear, a postal deliveryman, brought Smith's mail up to the Caledonia Tunnel he found Smith's badly-mutilated remains. A dynamite blast had severed and scattered parts of his body. The concussion had stopped his watch, conveniently noting the time of death as 7:30. Orear rushed down to the county authorities at Boulder to report what he had seen.

It developed that Smith had been last reported alive while buying groceries at Eldora. Following his purchase, the miner left town with his supplies in a canvas knapsack, apparently headed toward Hessie. When the coroner and investigators from the Sheriff's office reached the scene they first thought Smith's death had been an accident. Then the point of detonation was discovered, near the front portal of the main shaft, some 200 feet back from the place where the victim had been working. Blood stains on an ore car and Smith's bullet-punctured hat were found nearby. A trail of blood led to the point of the explosion, indicating that the body had been placed directly over the dynamite charge. In addition to dismembering Smith, the explosion tore a deep cavity in the tunnel floor.

In seeking a motive, the investigators discovered that Champ Smith had been a rather zealous fish and game warden who demanded licenses, even among his friends who occasionally augmented their winter larders with a vagrant buck. In this corner of Boulder County, few residents bothered with such mundane details as a license. When Smith took his duties seriously, his neighbors accused him of not being a gentleman. Acrimony followed.

Deputy O. B. Smith carted evidence from the murder scene down to Boulder. A diligent search revealed additional body and bone fragments and finally, the murder bullet. At Boulder, laboratory technicians fitted pieces together to form a skull, with a bullet hole through it.

Eventually Wilson Davis and the Smalley brothers were arrested. But positive evidence linking them to the crime could not be found and finally the men were all released. To this day Hessie's most famous murder case is still unsolved.

To see Hessie, take State Highway No. 160 to a point just a mile south of Nederland. Then drive west about four miles to Eldora. Beyond the town, continue on south, straight through town, to the point at which the road forks. Here, keep to your left, drop down the incline, ford the shallow stream that is sometimes there, and continue on into Hessie.

27.

IDAHO SPRINGS

IDAHO SPRINGS TODAY is a far cry from being a ghost town. My reason for including it in this book is a double one. First, of all came the photograph that accompanies this chapter. It was printed from an old but remarkably clear 7x9-inch glass plate and dates from 1880. I regard it as the finest early Idaho Springs photograph found to date. My second reason involves the early history of the town, with its inception during the very beginning of Colorado's mining period.

George A. Jackson was a native of Glasgow, Missouri, and was also a cousin of the noted scout Kit Carson. After an unproductive sojourn into the mining regions of California, Jackson returned to his home in 1857. Wanderlust and an appetite for adventure, however, are not so easily discarded in favor of the trappings of civilization. During the spring of 1858 he headed west once more, with the idea of hunting and trapping within the Pikes Peak region. After his abortive experience in California, gold seeking was not now one of his objectives. Yet history was to cast Jackson in the role of the original discoverer of placer gold in the Colorado Rockies.

When he reached the point where Cherry Creek commingles its water with those of South Platte River, Jackson made his camp near John Smith's trading post on the west side of Cherry Creek, well within the later boundaries of Auraria. For a time he bought and sold Indian goods, but he was soon on the move again. This time he entered the valley of the Cache La Poudre River. Quite apart from his avowed earlier intentions, he did engage in some gold prospecting here. Before leaving he also founded a trading post called LaPorte, north of present Fort Collins.

By August he had moved south again. Here, in company with Jim Sanders and Tom Golden, he prospected in the vicinity of St. Vrain Creek and the Vasquez Fork, later known as Clear Creek. When cold weather appeared imminent, the three partners established their winter quarters near present Lookout Mountain, about where the present city of Golden stands. Golden, incidentally, was probably named for Tom Golden. By January, Jackson's inactivity had engendered a persistent case of "cabin fever." Incidentally, Golden was then known as Arapaho City.

At this point a mild variation in accounts crops up. In one story we hear that Jackson entered the mountains in company with an Indian named Blackhawk, while another version tells us that his two dogs were his only companions. In any case, his route took him up Mount Vernon Canyon. Arriving at Bergen Park, he found and followed a large elk herd, moving toward the brink of present Jackson's Hill. Below, at the foot of the hill, he could see the solidly frozen Vasquez Creek or River. During the next several days, Jackson descended to the level of the river and explored the valley. Moving along, he noted a rather dense, bluish mist emanating from one of the side canyons. Quite naturally, he suspected the presence of a Ute Indian village. Through waist-deep snow Jackson struggled to the crest of Soda Hill, peering furtively down through the trees to determine the source of the smoke.

When no savages appeared, he stealthily picked his way down for a closer look. There he found thick vapors pouring forth from a natural hot spring. Following present West Chicago Creek down to the point where it joins the Vasquez Fork, Jackson built a large fire to thaw the ground enough so that he could dig with his hunting knife. Using a battered tin cup as a substitute for a gold pan, he began washing the dirt and gravel that he had dug out. When he stopped, about $9 in gold dust had been found. Convinced that he had made an important discovery, Jackson marked the spot carefully before heaping snow onto the spot to hide all evidence of his activity, a secret now worth his very life. After an absence of two weeks, he returned to the original camp at Golden. The actual date of the Jackson discovery was January 7, 1859. The location is marked now by a monument and plaque placed beside West Chicago Creek by the State Historical Society of Colorado.

By April Jackson was ready to lead a party of 22 men who had become his partners, from Golden Gate City, Auraria and Denver City, to his diggings. Since most of these men were originally from Chicago, the stream beside the Jackson placers acquired that name. In general, they traveled by wagon, cutting a crude road in advance of their route. In those locations where road construction seemed impossible, the wagons were unloaded, taken apart and back-packed by the men over the more difficult terrain. On the opposite side, the process was reversed, supplies were loaded again and the journey continued. Their arrival at the spot Jackson had located was accomplished by the first week of May.

Without lumber, wagon boxes were torn apart to make sluices so that mining could begin at once. From their first week of work the men realized $1,900 in gold. When Jackson ventured outside and began paying for supplies at Auraria with gold dust, the word was out that a great discovery had been made. From that time on, his movements were closely followed, hoping that others might be led to his secret source of the yellow metal. Finally he told John Gregory about his find, and the latter agreed to meet him there. Jackson's diary relates how Gregory lost his way and took the North Fork of Clear Creek instead of the South. In this way Gregory stumbled upon the great gulch that later bore his name and ultimately upon the first discovery of lode gold in Colorado.

Meanwhile, back across the hills on Chicago Creek, Jackson

had sold out his interest in the placer and had returned to his old cronies at Golden. In the spring of 1860 the restless Jackson showed up for the gold excitement in California Gulch. One year, however, was enough time in one place. April of 1861 found him back in Missouri. In later years he enlisted in the Confederate Army and commanded a division called the Arizona Sharpshooters. After the war he returned to Colorado and lived for a time in Ouray County.

Jackson Bar, as it was now called, was already a crowded place by May of 1859. Inevitably, a townsite was staked out. In the beginning it was sometimes called Idaho Bar. Later it was known as Sacramento City, Idaho City, Idaho, and finally as Idaho Springs. The general altitude of the town was about 8,000 feet. In general, the placer mines created little or no new excitement after 1862. When new lodes or veins were found in Virginia Canyon, a toll wagon road was opened to make connections with Russell Gulch, Central City and Nevadaville, in nearby Gilpin County.

Although the mineral springs that had attracted George Jackson were temporarily forgotten in the gold excitement, their eclipse was short lived. When Jackson first happened upon the springs early in January of 1859, the entire face of the canyon was buried in snow. With both Clear Creek and West Chicago Creek frozen, hundreds of mountain sheep were gathered about the spring for warmth. Later, of course, people also discovered the pleasing effects of the waters. Apparently the springs were not used for bathing purposes until 1863. In that year, Dr. E. S. Cummings put up a tiny bathhouse over the springs. It was used until 1866.

From the town, the springs are situated on a small tributary stream called Soda Creek, just a short walk from downtown. Chemically, the waters are chiefly made up of mild solutions of sulphate of soda and carbonate. Their temperature varies from 75 to a pleasantly warm 120 degrees. From 1859 until 1865, the region around Idaho Springs had been primarily a mining proposition. In subsequent years, the mineral springs formed an attraction for invalids and summer tourists. In general, Idaho Springs did not achieve its popularity as a summer resort until the years after 1870. Several rough log cabins were built around the site of the baths. In addition, the waters were bottled and sold in the east and elsewhere as a health item.

Another mining location, called Spanish Bar, was located on Clear Creek just a mile west of Idaho Springs. Activities here date from 1860 when large quantities of placer gold were taken from the channel gravel. Two parties from Iowa and Illinois respectively were among the original locators of claims' here. From the hill above Spanish Bar, a gold fissure also provided additional locations along its outcropping. In general, Spanish Bar was not active after 1861. Most gold veins in this country were narrow, rather hard and tough. Fortunately quartz lodes were located before the placers were exhausted.

In 1861, quartz mines were found in Trail Creek, southwest of Idaho Springs. Of these the Freeland was the most notable. Some of these lodes were considered to be tributaries of the Spanish Bar. Two stories seem to have survived in regard to the building of the first stamp mill. This honor is alleged to belong to a Dr. Seaton who came west from Louisville, Kentucky. His mill dates from 1861 and was below Idaho Springs, near the head of Grass Valley Bar. It was designed efficiently to reduce the ores from his own discovery, the Seaton Lode.

From another source comes information that the first stamp mill was put up by a somewhat erratic, eccentric and aristrocratic individual named Hart, who represented the Silver Springs Mining Company. Hart's mill was a 20-stamp installation, run by water power, and housed in an impressively large building. His personal residence and business office were combined in a stone house, erected nearby. The Silver Springs claim was a surface quartz affair with silver predominating over a lesser quantity of gold. After exhaust-

Here was Idaho Springs in 1880

In 1967, the town still had many original structures

ing their resources, the company gave up and deserted the mine. The 5-mile-long Newhouse Tunnel, now called the Argo, dates from 1892. It cost about $1,000,000 to drill through all the way to Central and Quartz Hill.

In the town itself, there were already about 40 assorted houses and cabins by 1862. Despite its identity as a combination mining camp and health resort, Idaho Springs was remarkably free from the sort of life that is sometimes associated with a pioneer environment. It was a quiet place. Two hotels seem to have flourished in the early days. The Rock Island House was built by William Hunter in 1861. Of log construction, it had only 3 rooms. In a second log cabin, just across the street, Bob Diefendorf and James Hamilton kept a saloon where gambling was encouraged and where fiery liquids were dispensed.

At the competing Beebe House, board and room were available for $30 per week. Under the circumstances, the fare was surprisingly good. It consisted of bacon, hominy, beans, bread, dried apples, tea, coffee, butter and milk. Idaho Springs' first postal facility was a simple wooden box, divided into little compartments. The most convenient location for the box seems to have been in the living room of Mrs. R. B. Griswold. If you were expecting mail, you simply dropped in to check from time to time. When George Patton became postmaster in 1868, a stagecoach line was started to connect Idaho Springs with Georgetown. Both passengers and mail were carried. Halsey Rhodes published the first newspaper in 1873. Although it bore the dateline of Idaho Springs, it was actually printed over the hill in Central City. Its life span was short. Then came *The Iris,* published by E. A. Benedict in 1879. It, in turn, was succeeded by the *Idaho Springs News.*

During the intervening years, enough diversity of interests, plus good highways, has saved Idaho Springs from an eclipse as mining decined. In fact, the Clear Creek County Metal Mining Association, with headquarters at Idaho

Springs, is the only surviving organization of its type in Colorado. To see the town now, simply drive west from Denver or east from Berthoud Pass on the new Interstate Highway No. 70.

28.

ILSE

ON MAY 20, 1862, President Lincoln penned his name at the bottom of an historic and far-reaching piece of legislation. This was the enormously significant Homestead Act, a law that made millions of Americans into property owners for the first time. Under the Homestead Act, any American citizen over twenty-one years of age was entitled to a farm tract of one hundred and sixty acres, without charge. The only restriction stated that the homesteader must settle upon the land and cultivate it for five years. At that time half the area of our country, more than a billion acres, still remained in the public domain. Since precious metals are usually found in mountain country and only rarely on farm and ranch lands, the discovery of gold at Ilse was one of those rare happenings, an unusual stroke of good fortune of the type that is rather uncommon in a farming country.

It all began ninety years ago when a Dutch immigrant farmer named Frank Andracich was plowing his land in the northeastern section of Custer County in the Wet Mountain Valley. Although the Andracich discovery is well documented, there is one account that credits the find to a rancher named DeLamar, under identical circumstances. At that time Andracich was turning the sod to plant a crop of late potatoes. Near the surface he encountered a strip of earth that was considerably harder than its surroundings. Further examination disclosed that it was a gold-bearing vein, about twenty-seven feet wide. Following the vein back to its

Collection of Francis and Freda Rizzari
Ilse and the Terrible Mill in better days

Collection of Robert L. Brown
Ilse is now virtually deserted in its remote ranch setting

source revealed extensive deposits in the mountain directly to the east of his land. After milling, this ore assayed $37.50 to the ton. In all, about 150 claims were located and filed. Of these, roughly 75 evolved into properties that were worked.

Beginning in 1878, a few homes appeared on the ranch lands adjacent to the gold discoveries. For several months the ore was shipped east to Pueblo. Later, of course, some of the men erected a concentration plant at Ilse, operated with water secured from nearby Oak Creek. Within a few years, the Terrible Mine had emerged as the town's best producer. Almost a decade later, its ores pinched out and production was curtailed in 1888.

Instead of seeking an immediate gain from the locations of known deposits, Frank Andracich spent both his time and his potato money in a futile search for the elusive mother lode. Apparently it was not here. Andracich, after exhausting his own resources, borrowed heavily from others. Nearly everything he attempted met with failure and in the end he ran out on his creditors. In later years, Andracich hit it rich in Idaho, returned to the Wet Mountain Valley and paid off all of his debts in full.

As a town, Ilse was never a large place. Notable among the structures that once stood there were three saloons, a post office, one general store, the mill, a hotel, and one boarding-house. Even in its best years, the town rarely had more than a few hundred residents. In later years the Grant Smelter people from Denver took over the mill at Ilse in order to get control of the ores. In its best years, this mill had a 300-ton capacity and provided employment for about 100 men. For many years the unrefined metals were carted out to Blackburn, 8½ miles to the east. From this latter point a rail connection with the Silver Cliff branch of the Denver and Rio Grande Railroad was made. Incidentally, Ilse experienced a second boom in 1903, but its duration was rather short.

Fire, the virtually unavoidable heritage of most mining

towns, swept away much of Ilse in 1887. It now appears that the blaze started in the second story of the post-office building. In most cases, the structures that were destroyed were never replaced.

Among Colorado's ghost towns, Ilse is one of the most accessible. Its location is still in Custer County, about 28 miles southwest of Florence. At the intersection, turn south (right) on State Highway 96 for two miles to Greenwood. Here the same road curves to the west. Go on for 12 more miles to the intersection where a Forest Service sign tells you that it is 5 miles to Oak Creek. At this intersection a good, back-country, graded road turns north (right). At the only fork on this road, go to the right and drive on until you come to the huge ore dump and mill which will be on your left. This installation and the few buildings across the road are all that remain of Ilse.

29.

INDEPENDENCE

MANIFESTLY, MOST FRONTIER developments and settlements are far too elusive to be delimited with any degree of chronological exactness. Fortunately for the present-day student of Western Americana, Independence is a notable and easily-remembered exception. On July 4, 1879, the Independence lode was discovered. Beyond this single fact, the usual confusion finds its way into the story. Charles Bennett, William Belden and Richard Irwin are all credited with the discovery in three different, separate and distinct sources of information. In this, as in so many other facets of Western History, the facts are nebulous but the original discovery is not.

At first, four separate camps existed in the neighborhood. Ultimately, a town grew up out of this confusion when all decided to merge with or were absorbed by Independence. Prior to the merger, an impatient crowd of miners built their cabins around the Farwell mining properties to become one of the "towns." During the comparatively short life span of the larger community, a multiplicity of names were employed from time to time, contributing still more to the confusion of those people who try to unravel the complex story from old records, newspapers, business directories, letters and interviews.

Among these elements of confusion were the following names. The town of Chipeta was actually only a post office of very short duration. It was called Chipeta in honor of the wife of Chief Ouray, government appointed chief of all the

Utes. One of the others was Sparkill (or Sparkell), which was also a post office which existed throughout most of the town's history. The last two were Mount Hope and Mammoth City. Both of these were names which came into use very late in the town's life span.

In the beginning, few obstacles could have checked the rush that poured in over Tennessee and Hunters passes. The Independence strike was made at a point five miles west of the summit of the latter pass. Later, of course, Hunters Pass bowed to the inevitable and followed the lead of the mine and the town to become Independence Pass. From then on 12,095-foot-high Independence Pass has been listed as the highest regularly used crossing in Colorado, despite the fact that its arctic conditions still keep it closed for more than half of each year.

Early reports of crossing this divide were usually thrilling, hair-raising episodes, but the richness of strikes on the Aspen side were thought to be even bigger, better, and more fabulous; hence worth the hardships. Many travelers rolled off over the steep embankments when the trail was missed in winter, and one man spent five days in an effort to get over to Leadville.

In March of 1880 the Twin Lakes and Roaring Fork Toll Road Company took over operation of the route. By May, thirty people a day were using the trail at a toll of 25 cents each. At one point in 1881, all the residents of Independence were hired to complete a section of the road that was particularly important to the Farwell Mine.

When faced by the growing need to house the incoming prospectors, a tent city sprang up and filled the bill until some more permanent cabins could be erected. The first general store, boardinghouse and restaurant were all conducted in tents. For more than three years, postal authorities failed to recognize the merger of camps and the Sparkill Post Office continued to serve Independence between 1882 and 1887. To be safe, business directories used both names. Forty business houses of various kinds flourished here in the 1880s, generally regarded as the peak of the boom. About 2,000 people are said to have lived in the town during its best years. In addition to gambling halls, it seems incredible that such a small community could have supported ten saloons. Nevertheless, the Colorado business directory for 1882 lists all ten by name.

Although not listed in the aforementioned directory, a "red light" district also flourished at Independence. At nearby Aspen, women of ill repute were rarely ever mentioned in the daily papers. One of the most interesting accounts in this field was left by a census taker of the period who admitted having some difficulty in properly designating the occupation of these personages during a morally Victorian period. The census taker tells us that the sporting women were averse to telling their real names or where they had been born. This is really not so strange since the relatives of many of them were under the false impression that they were employed as governesses, milliners, dressmakers or music teachers and that they occupied "way-up" positions in the society of the Rocky Mountains.

Independence, being a small and isolated community, also showed considerable ingenuity in devising various other means of entertainment. For example, one game involving rivalry on snowshoes was played to see who could make the best time traveling from Aspen to Independence. In general, their social, cultural, and esthetic aspirations were, to a considerable degree, imitative.

For some of the fruits of progress, such as railroads and cheaper manufactured goods, the mining regions had to wait until the eastern states had taken care of their own needs and were then prepared to shower their surplus blessings on the underdeveloped areas. Although no railroad ever reached Independence, it nevertheless felt the influence of the iron rails when they were extended into some of the nearby camps which had been built at a less rarefied altitude. Primarily,

Independence, photographed around 1900, below the pass in its broad meadow. Difficult terrain prevents matching this picture.

Many ruined cabins still stand at the site of Independence

the town was hurt when Independence Pass fell into disuse after the arrival of the railroads in the lower valleys.

Daily stagecoach service began very early in the life of the town. Shortly after the snows cleared, a concern named Wall and Witter began operating stages between Leadville and Independence in June of 1881. It was soon clear that their operation was a profitable one and two competitors soon entered the field. For many years, McDonale and McLain as well as Carsons Stage and Express Line, also ran their wagons and coaches up to Independence.

For slightly more than nine years, the town had grown and flourished. When faced by the need to retrench and tighten their belts, the exodus began. Some of the mines had played out and by 1888 the population was down to about 100 people. From then on, conditions went from bad to worse. Directly, most of the business firms packed up their goods and started down the hill. By the close of that year, all three of the stagecoach lines had discontinued their operations into the town. The post office, Ackermans General Store and a sawmill still hung on for a while. The Sparkill post office moved out on October 18. Between April and October of 1899, the Chipeta post office was active there but it was the last.

Toward the end, those people who still lived on the mountain decided on another name change. Independence became Mammoth City when the Mammoth Mine was discovered. A small boom resulted but other camps, in less difficult locations, offered chances for better returns. Scarcely more significant was the Mount Hope mine, unearthed during the 1890s. Instead of seeking a more original approach, the powers-that-be renamed their community for almost the last time. Mammoth City became Mount Hope. Since people generally are notably reluctant to accept change, neither of these latter names was ever popular. Finally, the original name of Independence was restored but nothing else came back with it.

There were some sincere attempts at reviving the town but none of them was successful. The Independence and Farwell properties were worked spasmodically until the turn of the century. In this, as in so many other camps, the mill continued to operate and was particularly active during 1879-99. Beyond this, a small flurry of activity revived some people's hopes in 1900 and again in 1908, but few on the outside took these activities seriously. Despite petitions, all of the mail for Independence was now secured at Aspen.

For nearly two decades, a pioneer named Jack Williams held out, pursuing a hermit-like existence. Shortly after the mill was taken out in 1912, he gave up and moved to Aspen. From then on, Independence—Sparkill—Chipeta—Mammoth City Mount Hope, became one of our most accessible ghost camps. Shortly after the town was originally started, the pioneers had said, "Gold is where you find it." By the close of its brief span of life, the last residents said cynically, "Gold is where I ain't!"

Almost a half century later, many of the original buildings still stand in their beautiful timberline meadow, just below the highway on the western slope of Independence Pass. An occasional hermit now and then moves into or out of the rubble piles but no permanent residents still call Independence home.

Like so many towns in this book, Independence is very easy to find. Drive south from Glenwood Springs on Colorado State Highway 82, through Aspen toward Independence Pass. Before reaching the top, you will see the town below the road to your right. An alternate route, involving a somewhat shorter expanse of Highway 82, may be taken by driving north from Buena Vista on U.S. 24 to the Twin Lakes Reservoir turn-off. This is Highway 82. Continue through Twin Lakes, stopping to see the terrible devastation caused by a very recent snowslide. From there, drive over the top of Independence Pass to the old town.

When the brush of autumn spreads its delicate pigments

across the high mountain country, this is one of the most colorful portions of the state, offering handsome panoramas. At Independence, one may photograph the old, brown, weather-beaten buildings against the brilliant yellow foliage of the fragile aspen trees, producing some startlingly colorful contrasts. Irrespective of your purpose, the ride to Independence is worthwhile, since enough of the old town still remains to make your visit memorable.

30.

IRIS

BACK IN THE 1890s, a whole series of towns grew up in the low, sagebrush-covered hill country south of Gunnison. Although Iris was one of the locations on the so-called Great Gunnison County Gold Belt, the town of Iris was actually over the line in Saguache County.

When free gold was found here by two men named Lehon and Turner in 1894, prospectors poured in from many of the older mining districts. Union Hill was the first name given to the town that grew up around the earliest mines. But the U.S. postal authorities insisted on a shorter name and Iris was adopted. Two versions of the town's naming still exist. In the first account the name is said to have come from the profusion of wild iris that still grow in the meadows nearby. The other explanation gives the credit to miners who called the town after Iris Heiner, 10-year-old daughter of one of the camp's most popular prospectors.

A road to Iris was started almost at once. Beginning in 1894, wagons found their way in and beat down a trail from the nearby town of Chance. Three times each week a courier from Gunnison brought the mail in over this same route. A single phone line from Gunnison provided contact with the outside. Several stores and a few saloons flourished along the single business street. Even though the population of Iris reached an estimated 1,000, there was never a preacher there to assist those young couples who wished to commit matrimony.

On Mineral Hill and in the surrounding gulches, an impressive number of mines probed the subterranean depths for precious metals. They had names like the Denver City, Governor Waite, Alliance, West Point, Tribune, Eureka, Gold Hill, Friday, Gold Sterling and Hidden Treasure.

But in actual fact there were few hidden treasures at Iris. The ores simply were not good. As a consequence, money for development was slow to come in. But for three demented summers it was Mecca. Then in 1879 the economic chickens came home to roost and Iris went into a decline. There was a brief revival in 1901-02 but the town died shortly thereafter.

Finding Iris can be a bit complicated. Perhaps the easiest way is to start on U.S. 50 at the eastern entrance to the campus of Western State College, the one across the highway from the little train. Drive east for about 5 miles, watching for a sign on the right which mentions a shortcut to Saguache. Just a few hundred yards beyond this sign, at a point just 5½ miles east of where you started at the campus, watch for a dirt road that goes off to your right, runs back to the east for 75-100 yards or so, and then turns south across the sagebrush-covered hills.

This road is bumpy, rutted in spots, and dusty all the way. When you come to the first ranch, ask permission to go through the fence on the road that leads around to the right of his buildings. In all you will drive through three fences. Be sure to close the gates again. In all cases, stay on the most used road. Far too many side roads go off in both directions for description here. At times the choice of which road is a moot one in a country where there are few landmarks.

Several ghost ranches can be seen along the way. Beyond the third fence the road divides again. Turn to your right here. Iris is just up the gully, around a few corners and over the next hill. If the weather is good and time permits, you could go on to the town of Chance, if you have a 4-wheel drive and are willing to backtrack from a few wrong turns.

Courtesy Library, State Historical Society of Colorado
The mining town of Iris, with the Denver City Mine at right

Collection of Robert L. Brown
The lonely and nearly empty site of Iris in 1969

Chance was just over a mile north and west from Iris and has about the same number of buildings still standing. Start at the water hole in the main street of Iris. Go left up over the ridge where the road bends around to the northeast. On top of the hill where the road forks, turn right and go down the gulley. Beyond this point you are on your own and good luck to you.

31.

JAMESTOWN

GEORGE ZWECK WAS ONE of the pioneer cattlemen of Boulder County. Without a doubt he was also the first white settler in the upper valley of James Creek. In 1860 he put up a cabin and ran his cattle on the acreage that would be the future site of Jamestown. While the cattle grazed, George got his jollies by prospecting for gold on those hillsides that were close enough to still be in sight of his herd. Although he did locate a few deposits, they were not very promising and the whole valley was practically dormant from a mining standpoint until 1864. Even then the situation did not appear to be very promising.

During 1864 some galena veins were found but they were not opened up to any extent since there were no markets at that time for this class of ore. Nothing else of any great value was found. Since the United States was embroiled in its fraternal war at this time, mining all throughout the state was in a slump. Neither materials nor the people to use them were available and the commerce of the prairies was being disrupted by the Indians who were charging about and doing interesting things to the undefended wagon trains. Nevertheless, about four hundred people gathered here along upper James (Jim) Creek and erected a makeshift mining town which they called Elysian Park. Two conflicting altitudes are given for this settlement. One says the elevation here was 6,920 feet while a second source gives it as 7,123 feet above sea level. Since both are close, the disparity is hardly worth fussing about. Anyway, this first boom collapsed after only three years.

After Frank Smith and Indian Jack found some good gold float here in 1875, a rumor started another small rush. Actually they had located the rich vein which led to the Golden Age, one of the best producers in the district. They later made the error of selling it for $1,500. On April 1, 1880, the inevitable post office was established. There was another boom in 1882 and this one proved to be permanent. Finally the town was plotted and everything was made official on July 25, 1883. Sylvester S. Downing was responsible for the new status and the new name of Jamestown. Downing was a county judge and a trustee of the town. He took the name from James Creek, chief source of the town's water supply.

There were two stamp mills in the town. The Golden Age specialized on free gold or gold quartz ores. The Buena was set up to treat tellurium ores. In addition to the Golden Age Mine, there were also the Longfellow which produced silver and copper; the John J. with large quantities of tellurium; and the Wano which was operated as a gold mine as late as 1940. During World War I, the Golden Age Mining and Milling Company turned its attention to the mining of fluorspar, uranium, and radium. From a financial standpoint, the output of precious metals from the Jamestown region has amounted to something in excess of $5,000,000, principally gold, silver, lead, zinc, copper, and fluorspar.

Jamestown had two principal streets. A network of smaller roads led up the hillsides, filled with small residences. When the first sawmill arrived and was assembled, the operators found it necessary to run it around the clock in order to keep up with the growing demand for lumber. About one hundred of the first stores, homes, saloons, and stables were turned out and literally slapped together in this manner. As an added attraction, there was a fine mineral spring close to the town. Many health-seekers availed themselves of this convenience.

Courtesy Library, State Historical Society of Colorado
Before the 1894 flood swept the site, Jamestown looked like this

Collection of Robert L. Brown
With a small resident population, Jamestown now looks like this.
Inset shows "short beer" check from the Rocco Saloon.

Two hotels, the Evans House and the Martin Hotel, sheltered transients and many people who worked in the town. By 1883, a school had been built and one church had been organized. Going from the sublime to the ridiculous, there were thirty-three saloons and dance halls in Jamestown that same year. A toll road from Boulder was in operation by way of Left Hand Canyon. Three times each week the stagecoach made its round trip up and back from Boulder for a $1.00 fare each way. From Denver, the cost of a stagecoach ride to Jamestown was $3.40. Incidentally, Jamestown was the hometown of Douglas Fairbanks, Sr., hero of innumerable swashbuckling motion pictures during the silent screen era. He later moved to Denver and tyrannized East High School before finding his niche in Hollywood.

Earlier in this chapter we noted that there were four hundred people at Jamestown in 1864. After the first boom had run its course, this total dropped to sixty-nine and seventy-five respectively in 1874 and 1875. In the later rush there were far more people who came and there is even a small resident population at the town today. In 1894 James Creek flooded and went on a rampage. Those buildings that were adjacent to the creek bed were floated down to Springdale and beyond. This was the same flood that destroyed Springdale. In addition, it took out roughly half of Jamestown.

Early in 1968 Jamestown broke into national headlines. On two occasions, separate caches of hidden gold coins were found under rocks on hillsides near the town. For several weekends thereafter the community had its own little gold rush as hordes of would-be treasure seekers invaded the area, turning over boulders in a fruitless search for more gold.

Jamestown hit the headlines again in June, in a Gilbert and Sullivan tilt with postal authorities. For some obscure reason a contract was let in faraway Washington to construct a new $14,000 post office at Jamestown. Residents of the town decided they wanted to keep their old postal facility, in the general store. Costs, they pointed out, were only $120 per year, while the lease for a new post office would be worth $2,000 annually. When the contract was let anyway, the protesting Jamestowners hired a lawyer and girded themselves for conflict.

As the David and Goliath battle lines were drawn, the citizens formed an organization called VOICE (Voters Opposing Indiscriminate Civic Expenditures). And the story has a happy ending. Jamestown succeeded where wind, hail, sleet, and gloom of night could not. It halted the U.S. Postal Department. On June 6, the department canceled plans for the unwanted facility. Jamestown's post office still reposes in the corner of the Jamestown Mercantile Company; and it stays open for 11 hours a day.

Today's Jamestown is a beautiful little mountain-ringed community. Paved highways lead all the way to the town. From a location standpoint, it lies in Boulder County, twelve miles north and three miles up from from the mouth of James Creek. To get there, follow State Highway 7 straight north out of Boulder to the Left Hand Canyon road. Turn left and drive for about five miles. At this point there is a junction. The left fork soon becomes a dirt road and leads up to Ward. For Jamestown, turn right and drive three miles. You will find a few stores still open, many original buildings, and lots of very friendly and helpful people. In a historical sense, Jamestown has survived a long and useful life, ranging from being a cattle pasture, through an existence as a mining town, to a placid twentieth century mountain village of great charm and historical importance.

32.

LINCOLN CITY

HARRY FARNCOMB HAD MIGRATED into the Blue River Country during the great rush to Breckenridge in the 1860s. Shortly after his arrival, Farncomb moved on up French Gulch in a search for precious metals. Frank Hall, in his *History of Colorado,* tells us that this area was named for a Canadian named French Pete who had lived in the gulch during 1860. While engaged in placer mining near the head of French Gulch, Harry Farncomb encountered some unusual formations of crystallized gold that looked like twisted or tangled wire. From then on, he spent his time in a careful search for the source. Quite commonly such specimens have washed down from nearby mountains. Within a few days he had localized his quest to the hill immediately above his placer claim. Here in fact was the source of his "wire patch" gold. For the next several months, Farncomb proceeded to quietly buy all available land on the hill.

News of his discovery spread quickly and the previously unnamed summit soon became Farncomb Hill. To accommodate the crowds who came up to mine, a small settlement called Paige City mushroomed into existence. When it became Lincoln City, the name change remained permanent until the town declined in the 1890s. George Crofutt, erstwhile chronicler of many early Colorado communities, listed a population of 150 people for Lincoln City in the early 1880s. He described the "City" has having, "1 store, 2 hotels, 3 furnaces, 1 stamp mill, and 1 steam powered saw mill."

Collection of Francis and Freda Rizzari
Here was Lincoln City, near present Breckenridge

Collection of Robert L. Brown
Little remains of Lincoln City now

The two hotels mentioned by Crofutt were the Whider and the Perkins. Various other population estimates have appeared over the years, ranging from 300 to 1,500 souls at the peak of the boom.

Mining in the Lincoln City area pretty well ran the gamut. Placer mining continued in French Gulch for many years after 1865. Several hydraulic mining companies existed in the area. Although a 9½ ounce gold nugget was taken from Farncomb Hill in 1869, the mines generally were not at all developed until the late 1870s. Most of the better properties were situated on Farncomb, Humbug, Mineral, and Nigger hills. This latter prominence has since been renamed Barney Ford Hill. Probably the most famous discovery in the area was another "wire patch" on Farncomb Hill, discovered in 1884 by E. C. Moody.

On the peaks around the town quite an impressive array of mines could be found. They carried quaint names like the Old Reliable, Country Boy, Minnie, Wellington, and the Cincinnati, where Spears, Conant and Company had a reduction works in place on the Cincinnati Lode. Earliest of all the mines on Farncomb Hill was the Elephant, developed by Harry Farncomb himself. Nearby there were the Governor King, American Union, Queen of the Forest, Bondholder, Boss, Bismark, Key West, and the Ontario, which dated from 1865. Down in the town, the Lincoln City Smelting Works was a very busy place.

One of the most interesting stories to come out of the Lincoln City area involved a conspiracy to wrest the hill that bore his name from Harry Farncomb. Before it was over, the struggle had acquired statewide implications and was called the "10 Years War." At one point there was a pitched battle involving 40 men who were entrenched in and around Farncomb Hill. For 7 hours, shots were exchanged. Amazingly, only 3 men were killed. But in the decade that followed, the financial gyrations of the warring factions broke one Denver bank. Finally the property was sold to neutrals and the strife ended.

Rev. John L. (Father) Dyer, most energetic of the Methodist circuit riders, lived in Lincoln City during 1862-63. At that time he had been placed in charge of the Blue River Methodist Mission. To provide shelter for himself, Dyer bought an 18 foot square cabin with an earthen floor. Inside, he put up a pine pole bunk. A quantity of sacked hay served as his mattress. For the culinary arts, he had 6 tin plates, a coffee pot, a cook pot, and a crude table. At one point during his Lincoln City residence he preached 7 times in two weeks. Frequently the sermon was given in his own house.

Since it was not always customary to pass the hat, Fr. Dyer kept the wolf from the door by carrying the mail on snowshoes. At one time he served as the deputy county assessor, earning $50 which he couldn't collect until 2 years later.

"The Sabbath in a mining camp," Dyer once observed, "was a high day for wickedness." Sometimes when his pants began to wear thin, he remarked that, "the boys had been rather long between collections." He noted that, "men would frequently go into bars to drink and play at cards when moral and religious restraints were absent." Incidentally, Rev. Dyer preached in and maintained congregations simultaneously at Parkville (Georgia Gulch), American Gulch, Galena Gulch, Delaware Flats, Gold Run, Mayo Gulch, Fairplay, Breckenridge, Alma, Montgomery and Buckskin Joe.

Lincoln City declined in the early 1890s. By 1893, only 25 people were listed as residing there. By the time the 1895 directory had been published, Lincoln City was not even listed. Today, the crumbling remains of a very few buildings still may be seen at Lincoln City. The site, however, is not marked. To find it, drive 4 miles up Lincoln Gulch out of Breckenridge. If in doubt, compare what you find with the accompanying photographs. They were made from a point just beyond the town, looking back down the gulch toward Breckenridge.

33.

LONDON JUNCTION

ALTHOUGH THIS TOWN has been referred to variously as Park City and Alma Station, its correct identification was London Junction. Park City was beyond it, at a higher elevation in Mosquito Gulch. Alma Station was a colloquial description that grew up in railroading circles. The Colorado State Business Directory for 1884 called it London Junction as does Mac Poor in his *Denver, South Park, and Pacific.* Flowers' map of Colorado for 1898 and the Rand McNally map of 1906 both concur.

In the valley above were the great London Mines, first located in 1883, and sources of the town's name. In the early days, a British syndicate from London, England, had owned these properties. Later they were chartered in New York and at Fairplay. Although never formally incorporated, there were one hundred and fifty people in town by 1884 and the peak was reached some years later when three hundred hardy souls had settled there. For several of the earlier years, all mail deliveries came through the post office at Alma. Later, of course, London Junction had its own post office. At the beginning, there were small clusters of log cabins and a few slab-sided structures here where Mosquito Creek flows into the South Platte River. In the course of time, a large hotel and a stagecoach station were added. For many years, the McLaughlin Stagecoach lines ran trips from Fairplay and Alma with transfers by way of London Junction.

Within a few years after the silver boom had started across

the range at Leadville, heavy traffic once again began using lofty Mosquito Pass and trade between Fairplay and Leadville was brisk. Since London Junction occupied a spot along the main road between these two towns, it profited from the exchange of goods and the traffic in ores. To assure their participation in profits from the ores being hauled over the range and to provide for a more economical treatment of their own mineral output, the London Mines Company put up a 20 stamp mill at London Junction.

Inevitably, under these conditions, pressure began to build up for construction of some sort of railroad between Fairplay and Leadville. Most of the agitation originated with the South Park side of the range. The *Fairplay Flume* pressed for the laying of tracks over the somewhat lower Weston Pass in case it was proved impossible for crews to put their high irons over Mosquito Pass itself. If all else failed, there was always the prospect of a tunnel under the Mosquito Range. Viewed in retrospect, all three of these ideas present formidable obstacles. Quite apart from the practical realities of the situation, matters got out of hand and a railroad was actually started.

It all began in February of 1882 when organizational procedures were undertaken. For lack of a better title, it was decided to call the venture the London, South Park, and Leadville Railroad. Among its notable sponsors were Hugh J. Jewett, president of the Erie Railway, George Blanchard, and Herbert Smith of New York. Bids were let, ties were cut, steel rails were ordered, and actual construction was underway in the early spring of 1882. During the warm months of summer, a six mile spur line was started from London Junction, progressing rapidly up Mosquito Gulch toward the London Mines.

Almost at once, a railroad terminal was constructed at London Junction. In its stock prospectus, the railroad stated its primary objective in a slightly different way. Instead of seeking to move ores from Leadville to Fairplay, this document said that the London, South Park, and Leadville was being built, "to transport the London's ores to Leadville via a tunnel under Mosquito Pass or over the top via the most feasible route." One source tells us that the spur line up Mosquito Gulch was eight miles long instead of the previously stated six. For more than six months the work continued.

By October of 1882, the track was completed to a point just below the London Mine itself. From this point, a 4,500-foot-long wire tramway ran from the mine opening down to the terminus of the railroad. Curiously, no additional trackage was ever attempted beyond this end of the line. All dreams of an underground tunnel or an alpine crossing of the Mosquito Range were abandoned. At the opposite end, down at London Junction, a connection was made with the narrow gauge Denver, South Park and Pacific Railroad. Taken as a whole, this combined railroad connection served to terminate nearly all staging in South Park and over Mosquito Pass. Incidentally, the gulch railroad spur was abandoned when the London Mine closed down in 1884.

A few additional items concerning London Junction also turned up during my research. Two of these which I cannot substantiate report the Colorado and Southern having extended tracks for four miles northwest from Fairplay to London Junction.

To see what remains at the site, drive out of Fairplay on Colorado State Highway 9 toward Alma. At a point roughly four miles beyond the town, a dirt road up Mosquito Gulch cuts off to the left toward the mountains. Here, just beyond the bridge where the road twists around, you will see a cluster of buildings. Some of these were a part of the original town of London Junction. This dirt road that branches off to the left through the town and up Mosquito Gulch was originally designated as Colorado State Highway 300, but many years have passed since anyone took note of

This early picture of London Junction shows only the closest mountains

London Junction, between Alma and Fairplay, is still there

it in this connection. London Junction was only a very small town, was never formally incorporated, and met its demise largely as a result of the mining collapse and the subsequent abandonment of the railroad.

34.

LUDLOW

It was coal, not gold or silver, that motivated the founding of a series of mining camps in the Ludlow Valley of Las Animas County, south of Walsenburg. Coal deposits within what is now Colorado were first discovered by Major W. H. Emory of the U.S. Topographical Engineers when he passed through southern Colorado in 1846. Coal, in paying quantities, has been found at a rather wide variety of places within the present boundaries of the state. Very fine grades of coal were mined at Crested Butte, Floresta, Lafayette, Como, King City, Louisville, and at several locations in southern Colorado. In the Ludlow Valley, coal camps bore names like Hastings, Delagua, Gulnare, and Aguilar. Ludlow was one of this group. Here was found a hard, extremely dense coal, much desired for fueling locomotives and for smelting ores.

In terms of size and importance, Ludlow would hardly qualify as anything more than a speck on the maps of its day. Sociologically, this was a company town, owned and operated by the Colorado Fuel and Iron Company. Company-owned housing, of a rather miserable "shantytown" variety, was available to workers and their families.

Although life here was started somewhat earlier, Ludlow first appears in the Colorado State Business Directory in 1911. It had a population of 50 people. John Allen was listed as the postmaster. Considering the limited population, Ludlow had a surprising number of businesses. Among them were a livery and feed store, two meat markets, one physician, two grocery stores, a justice of the peace, five saloons, a blacksmith, one general merchandise house, a notary public, a boardinghouse, and a fine brick railroad station. Ludlow had both telephone and telegraph facilities.

The 1913 Directory shows even more businesses. In addition to those listed in 1911, Ludlow now had a bakery, a stage line, a dairy, a book and stationery store, and one brewery. Curiously, the 1925 Directory lists Ludlow's population at 700, a rather unlikely figure.

Ludlow's importance in Colorado's history is not a pleasant story. Reviewing some of the background events that helped to bring matters to the brink of disaster at Ludlow may help in understanding the later tragedy. During the latter part of the second half of the nineteenth century, Colorado's economy was in the throes of changing over from a mining-agricultural economy to one that assigned an increasingly important role to manufacturing. Coal deposits, abundant in Las Animas County, became vital as fuel for the fires of industry. By the 1890s, nearby Huerfano County alone had 256,000 acres of coal-producing land. In Las Animas County, the Raton coal fields covered 1,300 square miles. The Colorado and Southeastern Railroad extended their tracks up the valley in 1904 and through the several mining camps in order to move coal to market. This railroad had no passenger service.

With profits to the operators running at a high level while living and working conditions for the miners left much to be desired, trouble was almost inevitable. Labor strife at Ludlow began with a first strike in 1903. At issue were living conditions, long hours, low wages and hazardous working conditions in the mines. Coal mining was, and still is, a hazardous occupation. Smog was a constant and accepted condition of life in the coal camps. Black smoke poured out night and day from the pits producing a smog-cover that almost never allowed the sun to reach Ludlow. As a result of breathing the ever-present coal dust, the life span of a miner was reduced to an average of about 45 years. Both workers and owners accepted this decreased longevity as just another condition of life. After completing a ten hour work shift in the hot pits the emerging miner was blackened from the quantities of dust imbedded in his dried perspiration. Red-rimmed eyes, ingrained with coal pumice, were a trademark of the miner.

For a variety of reasons the first strike failed. Not quite a decade later, trouble began again. Conditions had not improved. At issue this time were the ever-present work hazards, low wages, and long hours in the hot, sweaty underground tunnels. Squalid company housing still added to the discontent. Like so many other company operations in this era, the management at Ludlow paid their workers in script instead of money. This script, of course, was redeemable only at the company-owned store, where prices to the consumer, and profits to the management, were higher. The miners wanted the right to trade in Walsenburg or Trinidad, rather than in the company store.

About 1,200 men went on strike in 1913. Union organizers, under John Lawson, arrived to organize the miners and to help them realize some of their demands. In reprisal, the Colorado Fuel and Iron Company evicted striking miners and their families from the company-controlled houses. For shelter, a tent city was set up near the Ludlow railroad station. In all, this colony contained 275 tents and housed some 800 to 1,200 persons. Louis Tikas, a miner of Greek extraction, was the leader of the tent colony.

To put down the occasional fighting which broke out, the State Militia was called to the Ludlow Valley. The troops remained through several uneventful months, until funds ran out and some of the troopers returned to Denver. To fill the ranks, professional thugs were hired by the company and transported to Ludlow. One detachment of guardsmen was encamped about a quarter of a mile from the Ludlow tent colony.

On April 19, 1914, military officers rode into the miners' camp and demanded that the people surrender a boy whom they believed to be in the camp. Tikas denied that the youngster was there, and stated furthermore that he had never been there. The same demand and subsequent denial were repeated the next day. Tempers grew short. Expecting trouble, the miners had placed themselves along the railroad bed and behind the low hills around the tents. At that point the militia charged and the shooting began. Each side maintained that the other had started the shooting.

Fearing for the safety of their women and children, the miners tried to draw the fire of the military away from the tent colony. Militia machine guns raked the camp. The guns of the strikers were no match for the well-equipped National Guard. As a next step, the soldiers set fire to many of the tents. To escape the blazing canvas, the women and children ran outside. Some of them were gunned down in cold blood.

Other women and children sought refuge in dirt storage cellers, dug beneath their tents in anticipation of a long winter. Eleven children and two women met death by suffocation in a hole beneath a Ludlow tent. Louis Tikas was captured by the militia and was murdered while in their custody. In all, the fight lasted for fourteen hours. In the end, the strikers' ammunition began to run low and they were forced to retreat to the Black Hills, east of Ludlow. Wives of ranchers in the Ludlow area were terrorized by the militia because in some cases, they had harbored miners and their families for a few days.

When it was over, twenty strikers and their families and thirteen militiamen were dead. Ludlow's straggling survivors gathered at the Trades Assembly Hall in Trinidad. A dramatic mass funeral followed, with black-hatted coachmen drawing the coffins along the streets of Trinidad.

Ludlow is a bleak and lonely place today. It declined when coal mining ceased to be economical. To see Ludlow, drive

Collection of Fred and Jo Mazzulla
The Ludlow tent colony before the 1914 fire

Collection of Robert L. Brown
Here is the tent colony site at present

south from Pueblo on U.S. Highway 85-87 through Walsenburg and Aguilar. South of Aguilar, a marker on the right (west) side of the road directs you into Ludlow. A dirt road now follows the valley. At Ludlow, a few buildings are still standing. Near the site of the old railroad station is a monument which marks the infamous Black Hole where the miners' wives and children suffocated during the fire which razed the tent colony.

35.

MANHATTAN

THE FACT THAT GOLD existed in the mountains west of Fort Collins was first demonstrated in 1885 when specimens of the yellow metal were found at the Elkhorn Mine near the soon-to-be-established community of Manhattan. When the Zimmerman brothers, operators of the mine, exhibited their gold at the F. H. Burnett store in Fort Collins, an excited crowd of people swarmed around to catch a glimpse of the six retorts filled with crude gold. Judge Jeff McAnelly made a short, spontaneous speech congratulating the Zimmerman brothers on their success. Although the retorts were promptly shipped to the owners of the mine in St. Louis, their display caused a small rush of would-be miners to the Poudre Valley.

A double row of shanties was put up, flanking the single, rather wide street. Within a year it resembled the accompanying early photograph. As a town, Manhattan dates from September, 1886. From then on, "Manhattan or Bust" became a popular toast in Fort Collins. A druggist, A. W. Scott of Fort Collins, secured location of the townsite. In 1887, Frank P. Stover, secretary of the Democratic Mining Company of Fort Collins, wrote that the ore assays ran from $800 to $20,000 to the ton. Unless the foregoing figures were a misprint, someone was deceived. No really high quality ores ever came out of Manhattan.

From a mining standpoint, the rock here was granite, porphyry, lime and micaceous slate. Taken as a whole, the gold was found in true fissure veins. While the Elkhorn was absentee owned by a St. Louis syndicate, hundreds of other claims were filed and a few developed into mines by local people, sometimes at considerable expense. John T. Whedbee spent $3,000 in development work on the Emily and Monte Cristo mines. Then the district went into a slump and the town was almost deserted. Although things were quiet for the next few years, the end was not yet.

Another strike was made early in 1896. During the summer and through 1897, several parties from Fort Collins prospected quietly, making no mention of their activities. Gold deposits had been found again, this time at the grass roots. The vein was 18 inches thick. At the 100 foot level they struck ore that assayed $2,000 to the ton. Like so many other discoveries, the find was unexpected, and was located in an unlikely place. In a bend of the Cache La Poudre River where fishermen caught black bass, J. H. Gorden made the strike on his own land. The story became public when Gorden brought a large sack of his ore into town for treatment. In Denver he recruited miners and tunnel men.

When an unofficial census was taken in 1898, some 300 people had moved back to Manhattan. The single wide street, now lined with stores and homes, sprang back to life, becoming the focal point of the town. A stage line brought in new arrivals every other day and carried the ore and a few grumblers to town on the return trips.

But all was not well and not all of the malcontents had left Manhattan. Many of those who stayed felt that they were not fully appreciated by the Fort Collins' businessmen. Their appeals for aid and encouragement fell on deaf ears. When they requested help in buying a mill to process their ores, nothing happened. Perry Bosworth, leader of the dissident faction, said that the businessmen of the town did not seem to appreciate either the situation of the miners or the benefits bound to accrue to Fort Collins by the opening and operation of these mines. Bosworth, an optimist backed by a

The gold camp at Manhattan, 1888

Many ruins are still scattered among the trees at the right

quarter of a century of mining experience, felt that the mines around Manhattan would produce enough ore to justify installation of a 30 stamp mill.

But Bosworth was wrong. The ores did not last. Manhattan died of two causes. First, the gold was not of high enough quality to pay the bills. Second, high transportation costs for getting the ores to market ate up any profits that might have accrued.

Manhattan is in Larimer County, north and west of Fort Collins. Take U.S. Highway No. 287 northwest out of Fort Collins through Laporte to Ted's Place. Leave the U.S. highway here and turn west (left) on Colorado State Highway No. 14, following the Cache La Poudre River to Rustic. Here you leave the pavement and take an unnumbered dirt road north toward Red Feather Lakes. This road twists and climbs for several miles across ranching country. It ends abruptly at a stop sign where another unnumbered road, running east and west, crosses it. Turn left here and go a short distance to the first curve. Here, the regular road turns right or north again, watch for a rather poor dirt trail going off to your left. This trail follows a fence around into Manhattan's only remaining street. Beyond the fence at your left, nestled among the trees, are the remains of Manhattan. The actual main street ran north and south, crossing the present road just east of the previously mentioned curve. But only shallow foundation depressions remain at this point.

36.

MASONTOWN

NESTLED AMONG THE CRAGGY peaks of the high Colorado Rockies, one may still find a respectable number of comparatively little-known ghost towns. Among these smaller and more obscure communities, Masontown is a fairly typical example. When precious metals occur in very remote places, one of two things can happen. If the metal occurs in sufficient quantities, the world will build a path to your door. Toll-road builders, packing outfits, and railroads will become active, and the problem of transporting the ores to market profitably will be solved. But if the mineral deposits are scanty, the settlers embark upon a calculated risk. Perhaps with more capital and deeper mining, the richer deposits will be revealed. The point at which one gives up with calculated risks in the mining game has never been determined. Masontown was one of those towns in this latter category.

It all began back in 1866 when a General Buford opened up some promising gold and copper leads on a mountainside above Rainbow Lake. He began development work by building a road to his discovery, and soon found that a small village was growing up around him as word of his activities leaked out. By autumn he was prepared to put up an extensive reduction works. The fate of Buford and his plans remains nebulous. For some reason he seems to have dropped completely out of the picture.

Historically, the next development at Masontown occurred in 1872 when the Masontown Mining and Milling Company planned to erect the Masontown Reduction Works. This installation was built at a reputed cost of $75,000. It had a battery of 10 stamps, six Varney pans with settlers, a Dodge crusher, and a furnace of the Stuart patent. They planned to begin operating in 1875. In general, this firm was owned by men from Philadelphia and Georgetown. They leased the Victoria mine at Masontown. In addition to their own mill, the firm also put the old Buford mill in condition so that it could begin processing ore during the summer of 1875. If all went well, they hoped to erect still another furnace where they could add the Hunt and Douglas process for refining both gold and copper. All told, they hoped for a capacity production of $800 to $1,000 daily.

From the beginning, Masontown's greatest problem was transportation. The closest railroad was the Colorado Central, which ended at Georgetown on the opposite side of the Continental Divide. The Georgetown men in the Masontown Mining and Milling Company optimistically hoped for an extension of the railroad to the western slope. In the meantime, precious profits were devoured by the high cost of shipping their gold out over Loveland and Argentine passes. Later on, there was a railroad at nearby Frisco, but it arrived too late to help Masontown. In the end Masontown's demise was partially attributable to this factor, and partly due to a natural disaster.

Since Masontown never became very large, most of the residents did their celebrating down the hill at Frisco. On the night of the disaster most of the residents had left their homes to participate in a wintertime party given at the lower town. Just before midnight they heard what sounded like a muffled explosion. Higher up on the mountain a cornice of snow had broken loose. The descending slide outraced the wind with a cannonade of plunging rock and snow. Except for a few structures, the whole of Masontown was torn loose from its precarious mountainside position. Sleigh loads of

Courtesy Library State Historical Society of Colorado
Masontown, high upon a mountainside above Rainbow Lake

Collection of Robert L. Brown
Here are the overgrown ruins of Masontown in 1968

the returning revelers watched in awe as their former homes were reduced to splinters and then carried down the mountain in a chokingly fine directionless blast of snow.

Masontown was never rebuilt. Those last few surviving cabins were burned during July of 1968 since they had become a fire hazard to the expanding forest which has now overgrown the site. To see it drive to Frisco, west of Loveland Pass on U.S. Highway No. 6. From there a variety of back-country dirt roads can be followed to Rainbow Lake. Local inquiry will reveal which of these is in the best condition at the time of your visit. From Frisco, County Highway No. 1 runs south toward Breckenridge. Just south of Frisco a forest service road leads off to the west and goes to Rainbow Lake. In most cases, this will be the best route. Down at the west end of the lake, just beyond the Forest Service "sanitary facilities," a trail leads off through the trees. Although it looks like a 4-wheel-drive road, it soon becomes a hiking trail and is underwater at three points. Strategically located stepping-stones and a path make it possible to get around these spots without getting your feet wet. During the entire two miles to Masontown, the trail never gets out of the trees. Empty foundations, charred logs, and abandoned items of mining machinery are the only remnants that still remain at the site of the old town.

37.

MONARCH

NICK CREEDE HAD COME into the Sawatch Range from the east. While climbing upward his restless gaze quartered the brooding, darkening mountain ranges that rose against the tinted evening sky beyond him to the west. Below lay the wooded valley of the South Arkansas River, its stream a narrow trace, glimmering in the gathering dusk. Creede was a lonely, wandering prospector, little taken with the ways of civilization. After making a solitary camp for the night, he sat for a long time in silence, staring into the valley below.

Next morning Creede made a discovery that resulted in the founding of a town in this high, remote valley. The year was 1878. Unlike the settlement that grew up in Willow Creek almost two decades later, this town did not bear his name. Just what Creede discovered is still a matter of conjecture. It seems probable that he had been grubstaked by the Boone brothers, who were among the early-day road builders in this district.

From one source we hear that Creede had both the Monarch and the Little Charm mines, while another informs us that his mine was the Madonna. Allegedly, he gave the Madonna away when it produced only six ounces of silver to the ton. All sources agree, however, that Nick Creede's interlude here was not successful and that he soon moved on. In a historical sense, the records show that the Madonna, Columbus, Little Charm, Uncle Sam, and Monarch mines were all discovered in 1878.

Following the time-honored pattern, a tent city grew up along the base of the valley. In general, the tents were strung out in a line parallel to the South Arkansas River. This cluster of crude habitations was soon given the name of Camp Monarch and a few of the people who had settled there dug in for the winter. When spring came the mines were still producing. Gradually the tent settlement gave way to log cabins and buildings of dressed lumber. Most accounts date the actual construction of the town as such from May 15, 1879.

As the town grew, somehow the earlier name no longer seemed appropriate and was discarded in favor of Chaffee City. This time the town took its name from Jerome B. Chaffee, first elected U.S. Senator from the newly admitted state of Colorado and a leader of the Republican Party. On February 8, 1879, the legislature had formed a new county out of the southern section of Lake County. This was also named in honor of Senator Chaffee. As Chaffee City grew, something between 100 and 125 buildings were put up.

In the business district one could find such establishments as Bill Goord's Palace of Pleasure, Frank Ozman's Gambling Casino, and the Eureka Hall. Three restaurants flourished in the town from time to time. These were the Saddle Fork, Welcome House, and Katie Finn's Hotel. In addition to a drug store, some general stores and 3 assay offices, there were also a few saloons. Their names were fairly typical of those employed by other frontier towns. Included were the Arcade, Miners Exchange, and Last Chance. Fresh meat was driven into town on the hoof, slaughtered on the spot, and sold for 10¢ a pound.

Population figures grew to between 2,000 and 3,000 people. Some new mines were found also. Among them were the Eclipse, Smith, Gray, and the Silent Friend. In the meantime, Nick Creede's old Madonna property grew prosperous and began shipping 30 carloads of ore per day. During its peak years, 300 men were employed in its deep shafts. Over-all, it produced ores worth $40,000,000.

On March 30, 1882, a tragic accident at the Contact Mining Company property saddened the entire community. John Broll, an English miner who had a family at Monarch, attempted to dislodge an unexploded charge of dynamite. Somehow in the process the charge was detonated and Broll, an elderly, careful and experienced miner, was killed almost instantly. His body was horribly mangled. The left leg was broken in 3 places, both hands were shattered, his back was broken, and his face was literally peppered with small gravel. A companion was slightly injured but survived. Broll's wife and 3 children abruptly left Monarch for England.

For several years a stagecoach line brought passengers up over the 9 miles from Maysville for a fare of $1.00. The original Monarch Pass (old Monarch) crossed the range at a point 11,523 feet high on the Continental Divide. It was built by the same Boone brothers who allegedly grubstaked Nick Creede. The present Monarch Pass is on the other side of the mountain and tops the Sawatch Range at 11,312 feet above sea level.

A branch line of the Denver and Rio Grande Railroad was extended up as far as Monarch, with almost the entire town gathered at the depot to greet the first train in 1883. On this initial run, the locomotive pulled 3 passenger coaches, a baggage car, and a combination mail and express car, up to Monarch. To gain altitude, the tracks followed two big hairpin curves above Maysville and crossed a double switchback at Garfield.

Within the town, a musical group called the Scenic Line Band played concerts in the town park on Sundays. During the week, foot races and baseball games were held in the same facility, appropriately called Monarch Park. When July 4 came around, the whole community gathered to watch the annual fireworks displays that were set off on the top of near-by Monarch Hill.

Although some gold was found at Monarch, it was principally a silver camp. When the Sherman Silver Purchase Act was repealed in 1893, the decline of Monarch began and never ceased until the town had completely disappeared. This was accomplished in two ways. First, the few remaining residents gradually burned up the old buildings, stick by stick, for their own firewood. Second, some years later, an ominous, writhing white avalanche appeared, moving down the barren slope of the mountain southwest of the town. Only a few foundations now survive.

West of Poncha Springs, Maysville, and Garfield, today's U.S. Highway No. 50 passes within a mile or so of the old site of Monarch. The Monarch Campground road leads down into the valley floor. From the paved highway above, one may look down into the actual location from a point adjacent to the big lodge, unfinished at this writing, standing on the south side of the highway. Old Monarch once filled the valley below you.

Monarch, viewed from the grade above Monarch Pass

In a happier day, Monarch once filled this valley

38.

MORLEY

IN A HISTORICAL SENSE, Morley has led a many-faceted existence. Beginning more than a century ago, Spanish traders and fur trappers cut the first primitive trails across a low point in the mountains of southern Colorado. Called Raton Pass, it topped the range at a mere 7,888 feet. Later, in 1846, Col. Stephen Watts Kearny led his Army of the West over this route, widening the trail into a makeshift road that led him to a bloodless conquest of Santa Fe. Still later, Uncle Dick Wootton moved down from his saloon in Denver and built a toll road over the lowest saddle in the adjacent mountain range. By 1865 he had established a toll gate almost on the future site of Morley. Uncle Dick collected fees and operated his road between 1865 and 1878.

Although the origin of the name Raton is obscure (it means pack-rat in Spanish), it seems to have been the generally accepted designation well before the arrival of Wootton. Later, in 1878, when Gen. William Jackson Palmer tried to build his railroad over the range, he called the crossing Cimarron Pass. It was a railroad that brought about the founding of Morley.

When Palmer's Denver and Rio Grande began to grade a right-of-way over the pass, they found that the Santa Fe had beaten them to the location. In one of those cruel twists of fate, it seems that the Santa Fe advance man had ridden the Rio Grande to the end of its tracks. From there he hurried up the mountain to negotiate the contract with Wootton.

When the Rio Grande man arrived, just hours later, the "horse was already out of the barn." With armed mercenaries on hand, there was a bloodless confrontation between the opposing construction gangs, but the expected fight did not develop. The A.T.&S.F. went to court, asked for and received an injunction prohibiting its rival from interfering with construction. Palmer, wisely, began building westward toward Leadville.

Morley, in the beginning, was a railroad station on the Santa Fe line, with a population of 60 company employees. Trains often divided here before attempting the hard pull over Raton Pass. Three versions of the origin of the town's name exist. The first seems the more likely choice. William Raymond Morley was a Santa Fe construction engineer and locator who laid out the railroad grade in this vicinity. He also surveyed the line over Raton Pass. The second version has the town being named for Tom Morley, a local coal mine operator. Clarence J. Morley, Governor of Colorado between 1925 and 1927, was just too late in terms of the town's chronology. William Morley, with his Santa Fe connections seems a more logical choice as the town's name source.

As a railroad town Morley lasted less than a decade. Its post office was discontinued on March 5, 1885. After that it was just a station on the line and things were pretty quiet until after the turn of the century.

In its next existence Morley emerged as a coal mining town. Using drift and slope entries, the Morley Mine was first opened up in 1906. Actual production began in February of 1907. Around the mine a fairly typical company town evolved. There were 109 homes, a club building for employee recreation, an impressively located church, and a grade school. One unusual feature of the company store was its design. Its appearance was suggested by the Ancient Acoma Indian Church at Acoma, New Mexico. In common with most southern Colorado coal camps, the store was operated by the Colorado Supply Division of the Colorado Fuel and Iron Company.

Morley's coal was a very fine grade of coking coal, vital to the production of steel. Located on the highly productive Raton field, the Morley was one of three mines that supplied coal to the steel mill at Pueblo. The coal was also widely used by the huge Santa Fe locomotives. About 1,000 tons of coal was produced each 24 hours. Peak production was reached in 1928 when 500 miners were employed there and the output had reached 500,000 tons.

The Morley was one of the few southern Colorado mines that was never mechanized. Underground methane gas, a highly explosive ingredient, ruled out the use of spark-producing machinery. Blasting powder was also taboo. Coal was always extracted by hand labor. The unusual gaseous condition also ruled out the use of mine locomotives or electrically powered transportation equipment for bringing out the coal. Instead, the company owned a top quality herd of mules used to haul the coal out of the shaft. A large company-owned barn for the animals was built at Morley.

Morley's decline was directly attributable to the general slump in the coal industry. In all, as a coal camp, the town lasted for about 50 years. Morley shut down its mine completely for a time in 1954 due to cutbacks in steel production at Pueblo. Three quarters of the homes were soon vacant. By April of 1956, all but 20 families had gone. At the Morley school, 28 children attended classes until the end of the term that May. The mine was closed for the last time on May 4, 1956, when it was found that the coal vein had been completely worked out. All supplies of workable coal had been exhausted. About 150 miners, and a like number of mules were now out of work. At the time of closing, the last significant production figures showed about 600 tons a day. Total production over the last 50 years had amounted to 11,000,000 tons. Most of the families moved to Starkville or Trinidad. While the older miners went on union

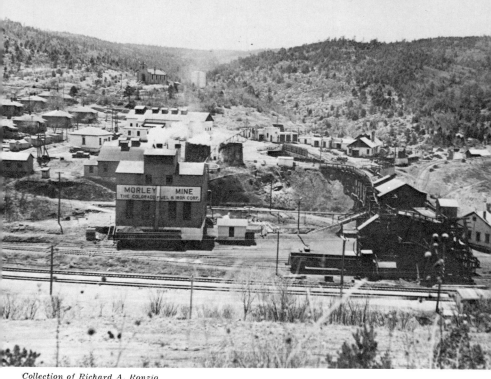

Collection of Richard A. Ronzio

The C. F. and I. company town at Morley

Collection of Robert L. Brown

The gutted ruins of Morley in 1968

pensions and social security, most of the younger men found employment at the C.F.&I. plants at Pueblo or west of Trinidad.

The location of Morley is in Las Animas County, on a hillside beside (west) of U.S. Highway 85-87, and present Interstate 25. Drive south out of Trinidad on the Interstate for 13 miles. On the northern side of Raton Pass, just before you reach the New Mexico border, watch for a whole hillside of ruins, dominated by a spectacularly situated church high on the hill. Between the highway and the town, the Santa Fe railroad tracks still wind upward toward the pass. Among Colorado's ghost towns, Morley is one of the most accessible, and it is certainly one of the few served by a freeway.

39.

OHIO CITY

ACCORDING TO 19TH CENTURY Gunnison County folklore, life at the future site of Ohio City could have dated back to 1850. When minerals were first discovered in this neighborhood an unusual inscription was found carved on a nearby tree. Under an 1850 date, a list of men's names was found, headed by a Captain Jones. From this event the location was named Jones Gulch. The Jones party may or may not have been engaged in mining. Since no other record of this expedition has been found, it is assumed that they were driven out by Indians.

The first mineral discovery of record was made on Dutch Flats, sometimes called German Flats, near its junction with Ohio Creek. The date was 1860 and the mineral was placer gold. However, no town was built at this early date. It was not until silver bearing carbonate ores were found on Quartz Creek in 1879 that people came in modest numbers and decided to settle there. Near the point where an old Ute Indian trail from Taylor Park reached Quartz Creek, a small settlement took root. Most sources place the founding in the late spring of 1880. In the beginning there were between 30 and 50 tents and log cabins there and the residents called it Eagle City. Late in 1880 the name was changed to Ohio City. For more than a decade the new town enjoyed the benefits of a prosperous silver boom.

Shortly after its name change the leaders of the community made a head count. There were 250 people there. With growth, a group of Chicago capitalists looked over the prospects, liked what they saw and stayed to invest heavily in both the mines and the town. Among other projects, they built the McKinney Hotel, Ohio City's first. As the town grew, fresh lumber was hauled down from nearby Pitkin. Soon a daily stagecoach service began running to the town from Pitkin.

Ohio City must have realized that it had really "arrived" when the phenomenon of crime raised its ugly head. On May 9, 1880, two men named Reed and Edwards shot it out in the street at point-blank range. It was the town's first murder. With continued growth there came restaurants, assay offices, a school, post office, general store, and several saloons that dispensed copious quantities of popskull whiskey.

Most of the mines that supported the town were located on Gold Creek. The Raymond Mine was the first in the district. In all it produced 7 million dollars, mostly in gold. Above it, the Carter property had a 1½ mile long tunnel and a huge 20 stamp mill. It shipped $3,000 in gold every two weeks and was a steady producer for two decades. By far the largest mill on Gold Creek belonged to the Gold Links Mine. It had 40 stamps. In all the Gold Links Property embraced 6,000 acres of mining land. For the 200 men who were employed at the mine there were many cabins and a large two story boardinghouse. From the mine opening a 4,000 foot long tunnel cut back under German Flats, intersecting a number of rich veins. Counting both gold and silver, it produced over a million dollars. The Sandy Hook was another good mine. The Calumet, Roller and Eagle lodes were within the town limits.

During the summer of 1882 the Denver, South Park, and Pacific Railroad completed its track laying from across the mountains and reached Ohio City. From St. Elmo and Hancock on Chalk Creek the tracks were extended through the lofty Alpine Tunnel. On its western side, the tracks crossed the grade of the Williams Pass wagon road by constructing

*In its heyday, here was Ohio City. Note Denver, South Park
and Pacific train smoke in the distance.*

Ohio City in 1969. Inset shows trade token from Wright's General Store

a series of rock palisades, rounded Sherrod Curve, and finally arrived at Pitkin and Ohio City.

When the Sherman Silver Purchase Act was repealed in 1893, the mines were closed and Ohio City went into a slump. Fortunately, gold was found in the valley of Gold Creek and tragedy was averted. During its gold excitement period the town adopted the name of Gold Creek. Later it reverted to Ohio City once more. A new hotel, the Arlington House, was built in the 1890s and the town got its first sawmill during this same period.

Although Ohio City declined with the deterioration of mining in Colorado, it never died. Today its population is about 20. It still has a post office, general store, and 1 phone. The location is 20 miles east of Gunnison. To get there take U.S. Highway No. 50 to Parlin and then turn northeast for 9 miles to the town, located just inside the boundary of the Gunnison National Forest. Gold Creek, the mining area, is reached by the dirt road that goes straight north out of Ohio City.

40.

PEARL

BIG CREEK PARK, the future site of Pearl, was first peopled in 1884 by the three Wheeler brothers, Luke, Bill, and Bob, and by a fourth man named Cooke Ray. Oscar Elms, the next person to arrive, took up a homestead in the park in 1887. The presence of copper, the key to the town's future, was first detected in 1894-95 but at that time copper was not considered to be valuable. Just five years later the discovery site was acquired by Charles Knapp, president of the newly-formed Pearl Mining and Smelting Company. Knapp had formed his company in the southern part of Carbon County, Wyoming, to purchase both Pearl and some other valuable properties nearby. Five million dollars in bonds were issued to cover the transaction. The copper property became the Big Horn Mine. In the same parcel, Knapp also acquired the Elms Ranch.

As a town, Pearl dates from 1900. It was laid out as a company project. The first post office was at the Wheeler Ranch. Luke Wheeler's wife, Pearl, became the first postmistress and the source of the town's name. Another version of how the town was named tells us that it was for Pearl Burnett, second daughter of Benjamin Franklin Burnett, founder of Lulu City. On the surface, the first story would seem to be more valid.

When prospectors re-entered the park in September of 1901, they noted surface lodes that seemed to be worth the effort of sinking a shaft. When this had been done they found not only copper but gold and silver too. John Telley located five claims in April of 1900. The Wolverine mine, across from 'the townsite and behind the smelter, had an 85 foot deep shaft and a 200 foot long crosscut, put in higher on the hill to strike the vein. It had first been discovered by Alexander Hilton.

Mr. G. M. Harding owned two groups of claims about a mile south of the town, near the Wolverine. The Copper King was also close to the Wolverine. A. Holroid and Associates had a group of mines near the state line, almost in Wyoming's Carbon County. The Lizzie Mine was nearly on the Wyoming border while the Grand Republic was south and east of the town.

Although the French group of mines was actually across the state line in the Grand Encampment district of Wyoming, the work and impetus for development came from Pearl. Most valuable among the deposits here was the Big Horn Lode, two feet wide and sixty feet deep. Charles Boettcher of Denver owned a large interest in the mines on Independence Mountain. From one hole near its top, $15,000 in fine gold was taken out. For hydraulic washing the French Group built a 15-mile pipeline to carry water from Big Creek Lake. At one point near the pipeline the Big Horn Lode was 4 feet wide. One unusual feature found at the Big Horn Mine was a fine steam hoisting plant.

Of all the mines associated with Pearl, the Zirkel (sometimes spelled Zerkle or Zirkle) was probably the best known. Over the years it was the scene of many rich strikes. Its lodes were fissures, imbedded between lime and granite. On January 30, 1903, a large vein of bonanza silver was found in a drift of the Zirkel, perhaps the most important ore discovery ever made in northern Colorado. As the exploration continued, workers broke into an immense vein so rich that company officials declined to discuss it publicly.

This discovery was in their north drift and ran from the 200-foot level. It lay 50 feet north of the shaft and some

30 feet north of the mineralized zone surrounding the copper deposits. Most of the matter between the veins was ordinary country rock without mineralization of any kind. Curiously, the silver vein paralleled a vein carrying copper but was an entirely different deposit. Copper is found in chiefly coarse quartzy feldspar while silver is found in very close-grained pure quartz, carrying only a small per cent of copper and pyrites. Some of the preliminary assays on this drift show returns of 250 ounces of silver to the ton, plus 10 per cent of copper Thus encouraged, the Zirkel people sank its shaft another 100 feet to open another level. With three producing mines on the same hill to the south of the town, little time was lost in building a smelter. The Zirkel was adjacent to the Copper King and Wolverine Mines.

Pearl itself did not resemble the typical mining village. Unhampered by towering canyon walls, its structures were spread out all over the meadow. Its streets adopted the names of its mines. Big Creek Avenue, Zirkel Avenue and Big Horn Avenue all ran from east to west. In 1901 only 50-100 people lived there, but with increased prosperity the town grew. One newspaper, the *Pearl Mining Times,* was published on a weekly basis. Surrounded by mountains and properly protected from the elements, the miners were able to work underground through the winters. On February 13, 1902, a local government was established and John Telley was elected to serve as Pearl's first mayor. When an electric lighting plant was built, the town began to buzz with excitement over a projected electric tramway connecting Pearl with Wyoming's Grand Encampment district. But this idea was forgotten in the face of formidable construction costs.

Among business ventures at Pearl there were two saloons, the Forney and the Hartzel. Three hotels, the Flineau, the Snyder and the Bulis, provided both food and shelter. Two Dutchmen, Van Duzen and Van Kleck, operated a general store in competition with the Townsite Company Store and the Smith Store. There was also a meat market, the Snyder.

The Pearl school stood at the eastern edge of town. Hill's Livery Barn and a blacksmith shop cared for the horses, and mules used in the mines. Among mining firms only the Pearl Mining and Smelting Company maintained an office in the town. There were also a printing office, a town hall and a post office.

Pearl declined as a result of exhausted mines and high shipping costs. Today the townsite is in the midst of an active livestock and timbering region. To get there drive north of Rand and Walden on Colorado State Highway No. 125. This road becomes Wyoming No. 230 north of the border. Cross into Wyoming and drive north just a few miles to the Big Creek Road which cuts back to the southwest and re-enters Colorado. At the first four intersections, keep to the left. In every instance these turns will keep you on the most used road. You will cross Big Creek between the second and third intersections. When you come to the sign which says "Big Creek Park 3, Pearl 2½," keep left and then right at the next fork. From this point a 4-wheel drive or a short walk is advisable since the trail was rocky and badly washed when last seen. I was told that you can also reach Pearl by turning right at that last sign and left again when you reach the state line. I have not used this route because of the prevalence of heavy logging trucks. Nearly two dozen buildings still stand at Pearl and remnants of the mill are yet in place at this writing. For the interested observer, much can still be seen at Pearl.

Courtesy Library, State Historical Society of Colorado
Here was Pearl, just south of the Colorado-Wyoming border

Collection of Robert L. Brown
Pearl is now in the heart of a rich farming area

41.

PICTOU

LIFE AT PICTOU dates back to a far earlier time than most of
the surrounding coal mining communities of southern Colorado. When people first began living along Coot's Creek
in September of 1887, the name of Sulphur Springs was
adopted. There were twenty-one of these evil-smelling mineralized gushers in the vicinity, hence this choice of a
name. From the very beginning, coal mining dominated
the economic life of the town. As additional drifts and crosscut tunnels were completed, the surface springs were drained
off into the subterranean coal deposits.

Thomas Lawther, an early superintendent of the mine,
was directly responsible for renaming the town. As a rather
homesick expatriate of the beautiful village of Pictou, Nova
Scotia, the nostalgic Lawther induced the residents to accept
the name of his former home. One source lists Lawther as
the first mine superintendent at Pictou. Since the original
Pictou is a French-Canadian fishing community, fronting
on the Northumberland Strait, it is difficult to understand
the similarity that Lawther is alleged to have rationalized
between the seacoast and Colorado's Greenhorn and Sangre
de Cristo mountains.

Before the turn of the century the Colorado Fuel and Iron
Company took over at Pictou. By 1902 the camp consisted
of some seventy company owned homes and a superintendent's house. Abraham Levy built the first store, a general
merchandise establishment, in the 1880s. Later in 1890, the

Colorado Supply Company bought him out. The Pictou store was the third one owned by this company in Colorado.

In the beginning, water for the town came from a fine spring nearby. Then for some reason that is still not understood, the supply failed. Some people speculated that its source had been tapped by a mine shaft. To add fuel to the fire it was subsequently found that underground water from the mines now maintained the former reputation of the spring, being both clear and pure. The Company soon established a reservoir above the town, large enough to furnish both the boilers and dwellings with abundant pressure for all household and commercial purposes.

Except for Sundays, a twice daily mail service was received at Pictou. Most outgoing mailbags averaged 75 pieces while the incoming load often included twice that number. George Tombling was the postmaster. In a busy office like Pictou, this was no "one man" operation. The volume of mail handled here warranted an assistant who also functioned as the cashier. His name was George Edmondson.

A Company physician, D. T. Baird, M.D., presided over both health and sanitation. Dr. Baird seems to have been a person with some other accomplishments to his credit. He also designed schoolhouses. One of his plans was so successful that the Company adopted it as their own and constructed "Baird Schools" in several of their other camps. In essence it was a double level structure. On the second floor it was arranged so that two of the rooms with a common but temporary partition could be thrown open to make one large hall. To assure being able to clear the area for any desired purpose, student desks were not bolted to the floor. To celebrate its completion on July 15, 1902, a grand ball was held at Pictou. In all, the school cost $4,000. One other reference in the Denver Public Library tells us that the fine school at Pictou was patterned after the Osgood School at the nearby coal camp of Rouse.

A kindergarten was a rather rare feature in mining camps

but one such facility operated at Pictou. Curiously, it was in operation during the summer months rather than during the more conventional school year. There was also a night school. Other uses of this school facility included a debating society and occasional health lectures by Dr. Baird. These latter would almost have demanded a multi-lingual person when one considers the sociological makeup of Pictou.

The population of Pictou would have qualified easily as a veritable turn-of-the-century League of Nations. Among the diverse national groups represented in this cosmopolitan camp were Italians, Austrians, Mexicans, Scotchmen, Germans, Irishmen, Swedes, Poles, British, Negroes, Russians, and a few so-called "native white Americans." One popular shift boss once found himself in a position where it was expedient to partake of several favorite national dishes all in the same evening. All had been prepared with great care by the wives of his men. Later that night he complained of a "multi-lingual bellyache."

A writer for *Camp and Plant* magazine, obviously a chamber of commerce type and far ahead of his time, dressed up the whole situation and noted that Pictou contained . . . "sons of Italy, señors of Spain, worshipers of Burns, descendants of St. Patrick, exiles from Russia, sons of John Bull, followers of Gustavus Adolphus and Kaiser Wilhelm, freedom-loving Poles, and besides the white people of our own land, some of the descendants of Ham." Curiously, aside from baseball teams, band concerts and occasional dances, there was little here that would pass for even token integration. Both a colored and a white boardinghouse existed at Pictou. Probably because of some of these unresolved differences, Pictou suffered from its reputation as a very rough town. Lacking even the most rudimentary intergroup communication, peaceful relations could hardly be expected.

Pictou's mines produced about 1,000 tons of fine domestic coal daily. Twenty-five mules were used to haul the coal from the pits to the railroad. Both the Denver and Rio

A view of Pictou, looking northeast

A few families still live at Pictou

Grande and the Colorado and Southern railroads served Pictou. In their common office, telephone and telegraph facilities for the town were found.

Pictou also boasted of a fine blacksmith shop and a machinery department. Here the Colorado Fuel and Iron Company manufactured all of the coal cars used in their various other camps. With a capacity of two tons each, these cars were made entirely of steel and iron. Several carloads of these units were shipped out each month. The C.F.&I. operated Pictou until 1912. Since then its decline has been more rapid. Although there is a small nucleus population, most of the old buildings now stand empty.

Just north of Walsenburg, State Highway No. 69 leads off to the west from Interstate 25. At a point about one mile west of the intersection, the town to the south of the paved road is Pictou.

42.

PLACERVILLE

THROUGHOUT THE ANNALS of the American West the name of Placerville has been a very popular one. Several of our western mining states have communities by this name. In all cases, the presence of placer gold in some nearby stream or river has resulted in the name. Colorado's Placerville is no exception.

In 1576 the 12-man Dominguez-Escalante expedition entered Colorado and camped near the base of Wetherill Mesa in present Mesa Verde National Park. They followed the Dolores River south; then crossed over to the San Miguel, which they followed down to the future site of Placerville. Beyond it, they crossed Dallas Divide to the Uncompahgre River. Their route later became the famed Old Spanish Trail.

Formal life here at the townsite began when a former military man, Colonel S. H. Baker, and a party of nine men left Del Corte in March of 1876. At that time the towns of Loma and Del Norte were the principal supply points for most expeditions to the San Juan Mountains. Following a still undetermined route, the Baker party proceeded to the San Miguel River. While searching its waters for indications of gold, they arrived at the point west of the Dallas Divide in May. Here their wildest dreams of quick wealth came true, until the placer gravels were stripped.

Baker and his men started the Lower San Miguel Mining District. When much exaggerated accounts reached the outside world, the nearly inevitable small rush into the valley was begun. By the end of the summer of 1877, a small town had taken root along the river banks. With a remarkable burst of originality they decided to call it Placerville. When the snows fell, most of the people decided to stay. Due to its generally low altitude, a mere 7,523 feet, the weather was fairly mild for a mining camp. Work continued through the winter. It is now estimated that about 100 persons were in residence here at that time.

George A. Crofutt, erstwhile chronicler of Colorado's early mining camps, visited the town, probably in 1879 or 1880. At that time he noted that Placerville was reached by a 36 mile trail from Ouray. He also noted that one could reach the town from Denver; fare for the trip was $30.45. Later, Placerville became the seat of San Miguel County. By 1881, the Bennett Dry Placer Amalgamator had started operating in the town.

Originally, Placerville was located at the point shown in the two accompanying photographs, where Highways 145 and 62 intersect, but it failed to stay there. Things changed quickly when the town was visited by an individual who wanted to start a saloon. History remembers him only as, "a man named Smith," and notes that he arrived in the set-tlement with a wagon loaded with whiskey and other appro-priate libations. After looking the situation over, he decided to locate his hooch emporium down the river, at a point ½ mile below the town. Inevitably, the whole thirsty popu-lation packed up and moved their town down to the new location. Soon there was a new general store, an assay office, and several single family homes.

The Keokuk Hydraulic Mining Company, the Mount Wilson Placer Mining Company, the St. Louis and San Mi-guel Company and, harbinger of things to come, the Phil-adelphia Cattle Company, all had headquarters in the town. By 1890 the Rio Grande Southern Railroad had reached the community.

Generally, placer gold deposits are not dependable for a

Placerville, Colorado.   Oct. 1887.

Courtesy Library, State Historical Society of Colorado
Placerville as it appeared in October of 1887

Collection of Robert L. Brown
Most of contemporary Placerville is around the corner, behind the prominent cliff

long-term prosperity. Unless lode gold deposits are discovered nearby or unless a new economic base is found, the placer towns die. When mining declined here, the livestock industry saved Placerville. Both cattle and sheep ranchers came in and established large spreads. When land for grazing grew scarce, trouble followed. In a violent range war, several sheepmen were killed before things settled down. In the years that followed, Placerville became a prime railroad shipping point for both cattle and sheep.

A disastrous fire wiped out most of the business district in 1919. Some of it was reconstructed and can still be seen today. To get there drive north from Ouray or south from Montrose to Ridgway. Turn west here and follow State Highway 62 over Dallas Divide to the sheltered valley of the San Miguel River and Placerville.

43.

PRIMERO

COAL, "THE STONE THAT BURNS," was the greatest economic reason for the existence of this town. Chronologically Primero dates from the summer of 1901. By October of the following year there were more than 100 small, single family dwellings. Primero had a night school and a library, both established by the Colorado Fuel and Iron Company, which looked after the welfare of its people and the town with uncommon paternalism by the standards of the day. For just about everybody, life in Primero meant a great deal of hard work.

Physically, the townsite was bisected by a large water system. The main reservoir was on a hill at the west side of the town. This installation very effectively separated Primero into an upper and a lower town.

In the upper part many handsome store buildings were located. Nearby, during its best years, the visitor could see literally hundreds of company type houses, brightly painted in a variety of attractive colors, a far cry from the dingy company towns of Pennsylvania or West Virginia. Here also was a club house, maintained by the company, where the men could relax in their off hours. Although people were poor by later standards, they didn't know it. There were no hideous slums and no one went hungry.

A neat double row of cottages, built along a single street, characterized the lower town. Most of the people lived in one- or two-story frame houses. Sometimes there were a front porch and a yard with shade trees and a picket fence. Life was comparatively simple, pleasures few. There were occasional Saturday night band concerts or lectures at the school. Sundays half the town went out walking. In spring there was fair fishing upstream from the town. In fall, when the aspen and cottonwood trees turned yellow against the pines, there was hunting on the hillsides. In winter there were sleigh rides, tobogganing parties, and sometimes skiing and ice skating.

Nearby, the tracks of the Colorado and Wyoming Railroad paralleled the settlement. Since coal mining was the principal industry, Primero had a smog problem. But except for those days when smoke from the 800 coke ovens at Segundo blew up the valley, life at Primero was pleasant.

For Primero, the railroad was an essential of life. By wagon road, the town was only a mile or so from Segundo. But due to the considerably greater gain in elevation between the towns, it was necessary for the train to travel 3½ miles in getting up to Primero. There were also good connections with the outside world. From Primero, passengers could ride 15 miles to Jansen where connections were made with the Atchison, Topeka and Santa Fe Railway. At Sopris, just 13 miles from Primero, one could transfer to either the Denver and Rio Grande or to the Colorado and Southern Railway.

In the town itself, families could hear the squalls and puffs of the tiny locomotives pulling or pushing their loaded cars from the coal-mines to the tipple. There the coal was dumped into larger gondola cars for the trip down to Segundo.

At the present time, except for a few favored localities, there has been a slump in coal mining all over America. Long, costly hauls from the mines, the popularity and cleanliness of natural gas, and the conversion of railroads to diesel power, are a few of the reasons why less coal is mined today. There is no shortage of coal. Primero, caught in the middle of a great industrial shift, was one of the dozens of similar towns that died. Today only scattered foundations, an occasional

Camp and Plant Magazine, from the Western History Collection, Denver Public Library
The once-thriving town of Primero on the Colorado and Wyoming Railroad

Collection of Robert L. Brown
Primero's ruins, at the head of Smith Canyon

wall, the abandoned railroad grade and the mines mark the site.

Primero's location is in the southern part of Las Animas County and about 17 miles west of Trinidad. Getting there, however, is difficult. State Highway No. 12 west from Trinidad will take you to Segundo. While Primero was only a little more than a mile to the north, the wagon road is gone and most of the old railroad grade has been washed away and what remains is now cut up by barbed wire fences. In short, one must walk to Primero. Currently the land is private. At this writing it is owned by the family of the postmistress of Segundo, a very gracious lady who gave me both directions and permission to walk in. If you want to go, begin here in this way.

Roughly, the directions are as follows: drive west out of Segundo about ¼ mile to the top of the first hill. A wire gate on your right provides access to a trail to the old cemetery. Close the gate after you and just follow the ruts to the burial ground. You can probably drive this far. Leave your car near the cemetery gate and start hiking toward the north, keeping the barbed wire fence on your left.

While the actual distance is just over a mile, as the crow flies, a whole series of deeply eroded gullies run east to west at right angles to the direction you must walk. After the first half dozen I lost count. By the time you have hiked down into these gulches and have climbed back out of them, you will have walked between 3 and 4 miles. Still keeping the fence at your left, keep going until you come to another fence that crosses the way you must go. Primero is beyond this fence, just over the next hill.

At the time of my visit, Primero was occupied by a herd of cattle and one very large, long-horned, unfriendly, and excessively noisy bull. Caution and prudence should be observed.

44.

RED CLIFF

FROM THE VERY beginnings of recorded history, the western
slope of our Colorado Rockies had been regarded as the nearly
exclusive preserve of the Ute Indians. During the first half
of the 19th century, fur traders and trappers penetrated
Western Colorado without regard for any prior rights of the
first residents. One of the very heavily trapped areas was
the Eagle River Valley. Both Kit Carson and John C. Fremont are known to have been active here. In those beginning
years, the Eagle was known as the Piney River. Fremont and
Carson usually operated as a team. Carson was Fremont's
guide on all of his western explorations except during the ill-
fated journey of 1848. These two men were responsible for
naming the Tennessee Fork of the Arkansas River.

When gold and silver were found here in 1879 and 1880
the valley was still a part of Summit County. All of this
changed on February 11, 1883, with the formation of Eagle
County. Red Cliff dates from this early mineral excitement.
Some reference can be found where the town is called Red-
cliff. I base my choice of the two word form on the authoritative *Mining in Colorado,* by C. W. Henderson. Geographically, Red Cliff is close to both Battle and Horn mountains.
Production of silver ranked first in the economy of the town,
followed closely by gold, copper, lead and zinc. Red Cliff
was built at the southern foot of Shrine Pass, where Turkey
Creek makes its junction with the Eagle River. Most of the
mines were on nearby Battle Mountain, named for a wild

melee that took place between the Utes and Arapahos way back in 1849.

As time passed, Red Cliff became the most important town in the Eagle Valley and ultimately the seat of Eagle County. By 1884 the population was up to 800 people and there was a post office. Among the five hotels, the National was the best known. With growth came families and a demand for schools. Growth also brought saloons. An opera house was erected in order to take advantage of the large number of touring theatrical groups, musical companies, and traveling lecturers then so prevalent in Colorado. A cornet brass band was formed to play at Red Cliff on important occasions. Churches of several denominations were also built. Some of them are still standing.

At first, Red Cliff was a part of the Battle Mountain Mining district. Most Colorado mining districts were small and the names were changed frequently. Over the years, this one was known successively as the Belden, Silver Horn, Horn Silver and Red Cliff Mining districts. In all of these instances the actual area never changed. All names applied to the same territory. Two newspapers, the *Shaft* and the *Red Cliff Comet,* a weekly that was once printed on wallpaper, kept the town informed.

When the White River Utes went on their notable rampage during 1879, fear of an all-out Indian attack spread southwestward into the towns of the Eagle Valley. At Red Cliff, a huge log fort was hastily erected to afford protection for the women and children, and any of the men lucky enough to get inside. Considering the distance from the Meeker Massacre site, it is not particularly surprising to note that the expected attack never materialized.

Nevertheless, the hasty construction of a fort at Red Cliff must be evaluated within the framework of the times. When we consider the fact that the American Indian really won more engagements than he lost, the stockade fort at Red Cliff was a realistic act. Quite apart from the Hollywood

Here was Red Cliff when George Beam visited the town

Here is Red Cliff today, still going strong

stereotypes of Indian battles, what the Utes did to Meeker, what the Sioux did to Custer and the way in which they defeated Crooke earlier at the Rosebud, the Fetterman and Grattan massacres, were all far more typical of reality than is the garbage that is being fed to the younger generation today. In general, when forces were equal, the Indian won his wars, but lost the last battle and with it his cause. Usually, Indians avoided attacking organized towns. The actions at Colorado City and the sacking of Julesburg were among the exceptions. Fortunately, Red Cliff escaped this fate.

During the early 1880s, the Denver and Rio Grande Railroad ran surveys up Homestake Creek with the idea of extending a spur line of their railroad up that valley. In the process, their survey crews found paying quantities of good gold float along the creek. These discoveries contributed enormously to the prosperity of the region and added population to the towns of Gold Park, Camp Fancy, and Holy Cross City. Red Cliff benefited too by becoming the commercial center of a whole nucleus of mining camps located on the surrounding hills. Although the Denver and Rio Grande reached Red Cliff, the projected spur line up Homestake Creek was never built.

Today, Red Cliff is a pretty little town, still standing in the bottom of its beautiful valley. A small number of families still live there. Its location is barely to the east of U.S. Highway No. 24, north of Leadville and Tennessee Pass, and south of Minturn.

45.

REXFORD

ALTHOUGH VERY FEW of the facts of its existence are known, Rexford is a gem of an example of the hundreds of single-mine towns that once were so prevalent in our high Colorado Rockies. Its state of preservation and handsome location dictate its inclusion in this book. Such communities were almost totally dependent upon the output of just one mineral property, usually a rather rich one. Rexford, like most of its contemporaries of this type, was a company mining town. The Rexford Mining Corporation owned the land and had paid for the buildings that were erected there. Rexford was listed in the Colorado Business Directory for 1884.

Although the company had holdings and operated in other sections of Colorado, this town was a sort of official head-quarters. The Rexford firm was formally organized as a Colorado Corporation in 1881. Rexford, the town, dates from that year. Capital stock in the amount of $100,000 was issued for sale to the public. In all of the building con-struction, the early-type square nails were employed through-out. Taken as a whole, Rexford was a very small town. En-tering the town from the Dillon and Breckenridge country, the first building on the left was the general store, con-structed according to the best western traditions with a false-front and big glass windows facing the town's single street.

Immediately adjacent to the store, a small log cabin housed either the assay office or a pioneer family. There are two opinions. Beyond it is another log cabin that was formerly the only saloon in town. Nothing except the walls stand now. Apparently the roof has been gone for quite a while since a tall evergreen now grows straight up from inside the cabin. The remarkably luxuriant growth of this tree stands in mute testimony to the fertilizing qualities of the products that were once sold in the Rexford gin mill.

Across the principal street one may still see the crumbling remains of Rexford's boardinghouse which also doubled as the hotel. It was by far the largest and most ambitious building in town. Behind it, a small stream courses through the meadow. In better days, it supplied water for washing, cooking and the other myriad necessities of life. Water for the mine also came from this same source. Another large structure stands a few yards beyond the town, just past the edge of the trees.

From this point, the remains of a wagon road start to climb up out of the meadow. On the right side, about a quarter of a mile outside the town, stood the Rexford Mine. The usual pile of smoothly polished rocks and a tailings dump now mark the site. All surface buildings are gone. The road goes on, up into the trees. An early reference in the files of the State Historical Society of Colorado tells how this road crossed the range to Montezuma and the Snake River settlements on the other side. In the early days, the road was used to transport both freight and passengers across the mountains. The sudden impact of mechanized transportation on Colorado mining camps, coincident with the flow of transportation into these areas, both speeded to a close the Far Western frontier and rendered more difficult and costly the orderly succession of an economically sound system. Twice weekly mail service also reached the town by this route. In those days there was even a post office at Rexford. It was probably housed in either the general store or at the hotel.

After a very brief period, the principal vein of the mine beyond Rexford pinched out. When this happened, the small resident population packed up its few personal effects and moved elsewhere. The migratory life of the miner was by no means as colorful and exciting as that of the cowboy but the mining industry in these hundreds of tiny camps scattered throughout the Rocky Mountains, was of very great importance in the economic development of the Far West.

If you decide to see Rexford for yourself, there is only one way to get there. State Highway 9 runs also straight north and south between Breckenridge and Dillon. Roughly two-thirds of the way south toward Breckenridge, an unnumbered dirt road turns straight east for 5 miles to Tiger. Beyond Tiger the road forks. The right branch goes up past the huge piles of dredged rocks to the old site of Parkville. To the left, the somewhat rougher branch bends around through a meadow, past a cabin and the remains of a house trailer before entering the trees. At its best, this road leaves something to be desired and it is better to be aware of the limitations of your own vehicle. When you get to the remains of an old bridge that looks like you shouldn't try to drive over it, don't cross it. From the point where you first see the bridge, back up for 50 yards or so until you come to a trail leading off to the left and up the hill.

Rexford lies about four miles or so up this trail. Along the way, you will pass three or four old cabins on the right side. These were constructed with round nails and are not as old as Rexford. Go on for about one more mile. As you emerge from the trees into an open meadow, the cluster of old weathered-brown buildings is seen. I have always preferred to drive to Rexford by Jeep. In one or two places the grades are steep and there are some spots where a vehicle with good clearance is desirable. This is not intended to convey the idea that a conventional car cannot be driven up here, but caution should be the rule if you try it.

Many large areas of the Rocky Mountain West could not be made to yield up a living after the mines played out. In the intervening years these same lands have never been taken up again by individuals. Thus the frontier line of settlement became a broken line in the Far West. In these abandoned settlements like Rexford we find the true genesis of the ghost towns.

Collection of Robert L. Brown
   Rexford, deep in the mountains, showing the hotel at right and the general store at left

Collection of Robert L. Brown
      The main buildings at Rexford. The saloon is at the left

46.

ROBINSON

In a historical sense, the development of Robinson dates back to 1860 when miners from Breckenridge crossed the range and worked a series of rich gold placers in McNulty Gulch. Before they were abandoned in 1862, the placers had yielded about $300,000 in gold. Beyond this, things were quiet in the valley until the rich boom at Leadville in the late 1870s. Among the overflow from Leadville were many who surged over the hills in a search for other indications of the same class of carbonate ores that had made Leadville prosper.

Here, near the top, on the northern slopes of Fremont Pass, silver deposits were found in what was to become the Ten Mile Mining District. Each new discovery served to attract new prospectors until a small ramshackle settlement called Carbonateville was established during the winter of 1878-79. At that time, 10 feet of snow blanketed the site.

Soon after A. J. Streeter had erected the first dwelling, Carbonateville became successively Carbonate City, Ten Mile City, Summit City, and Robinson's Camp. Frank Fossett described Carbonateville as, "A strange medley of log cabins, tents, and primitive habitations, and the prices of town lots compared in altitude with the places in which they were located." Apparently in the beginning, Carbonateville and Robinson's Camp were separate settlements, located a half mile apart. With growth and mergers, it became the chief rival of booming Kokomo, located 1½ miles farther down the same valley. When new roads between Georgetown and Leadville were completed in 1879, the entire Ten Mile District reaped the benefits. In spring, however, melting snow made the new roads nearly impassable. By April of 1879, stagecoach service from Leadville was already a reality. Sometime late in 1880, the town adopted a final change of identity and simply became Robinson, named for the chief benefactor of the town.

George B. Robinson was a Leadville merchant who, like many of his contemporaries, made a practice of grubstaking would-be miners in exchange for a share of whatever they were able to find. His involvement with the town that later bore his name began in the fall of 1879. Robinson had advanced mining and food supplies to Charles Jones and John Y. (Jack) Shedden in exchange for a half interest in any promising veins they were lucky enough to uncover. Although a 50% rate seems rather high, the risks were even higher. Most grubstaked prospectors found nothing. The few fortunate ones indirectly financed the failures.

Jones and Shedden located the nucleus of what became known as the Robinson group of mines. Robinson himself bought out the shares of his partners and moved quickly into active management of his new properties. He organized the Robinson Consolidated Mining Company, with headquarters in New York. The firm was capitalized at $10,000,-000. Robinson's properties included two of the best mines in the district, the White Quail and the Wheel of Fortune. Although he had been a Colorado resident for only two years, he had become an immensely popular man. In November of 1880, he was elected to the office of Lt. Governor of Colorado, barely satisfying the residency requirement imposed by the State Constitution. Robinson had been elected in November. Before the year was over, the town that had grown up around his mines had been renamed in his honor, and Robinson himself was dead.

The Robinson mines turned in big profits and the town

grew. During the 1880s its population fluctuated between 700 and 800 people. Governor Robinson built a fine hotel, the Robinson, there and financed the establishment of a bank and a smelter. A second hotel, the Bonanza, also flourished. Other improvements included a newspaper, a Catholic church, four sawmills, and a telegraph office. Soon the booming town had become the principal business center for Summit County.

In several ways, the story of George Robinson paralleled that of his contemporary, H. A. W. Tabor. Both men were Leadville merchants. Both grubstaked miners and acquired wealth as a chance result. Robinson and Tabor were both Republicans and each was elected Lt. Governor of Colorado. There the similarity ends. Robinson was not plagued with the Tabor variety of wife trouble, and he did not live, as Tabor did, to see the demonetization of silver in 1893. Robinson was killed at the height of his career.

The trouble began with a dispute between Robinson and Captain J. W. Jacque concerning ownership of the Smuggler Mine. Governor Robinson had placed guards, armed with rifles, around his property. His orders authorized the guards to keep out intruders, by shooting if necessary. On November 27 Robinson received a report that described how Jacque was planning to take over the property by force. That night he went out on a personal tour of inspection to check on his guards. There was another rumor about one of the guards being away from his station. In any case, Robinson went up personally to the barricaded door of the tunnel. For some now unknown reason he failed to identify himself. The guard, jumpy with apprehension and very much on duty, followed instructions to the letter. After asking who was there, he fired into the darkness without waiting for a reply. Robinson, struck in the side by the bullet, dropped in his tracks. Two days later, on the 29th of November, he died.

Despite this loss, life at the town of Robinson went on.

Collection of Francis and Freda Rizzari
Robinson in winter, with a Denver and Rio Grande Railroad train

Collection of Robert L. Brown
This dump now covers the site of Robinson

The Denver and Rio Grande Railroad laid tracks in the snow during the winter of 1880-81. On New Year's Day, 1881, their first train rolled into Robinson as a part of a huge celebration heralding the arrival of progress. The Denver and South Park Railroad built into Summit County during August of 1882. Two sets of tracks, a high and a low line, nearly paralleled each other through the town.

Robinson's ores were exhausted in the early 1890s. When the Sherman Silver Purchase Act was repealed in 1892, the end of Robinson was in sight. Although some families continued to live there for many years, the great days were over. There was a slight flurry of activity in the 1920s when gold was found in McNulty Gulch, but the supply did not prove adequate to justify a resurgence of the town.

Today, the beautiful valley that once held the town of Robinson is buried under tons of silt from the nearby mills of the Climax Molybdenum Company. Some years ago the Climax Company purchased the empty townsite, disinterred the graves from the old cemetery, and began dumping their waste into the valley. Now, only the tops of the mountains that showed in old pictures, can still be seen above the deep sea of blowing silt.

For those interested in the actual location, one may drive west on U.S. Highway No. 6 and the new Interstate 70 over Loveland Pass to Frisco. Where the road forks beyond the town, drive south on State Highway 91 for five miles toward Fremont Pass. At that point, look off to your right or east. The remains of Robinson are forever buried under the dump that now fills the valley below you.

47.

ROUSE

THERE WERE TWO of these towns, both coal mining camps in Huerfano County, and both bore the name of Rouse. To avoid confusion the first one, established in the 1880s, was called Old Rouse. It was abandoned in 1900 and the residents simply moved themselves and their homes to New Rouse, just a few miles away on Santa Clara Creek. At Old Rouse, only scars remain.

Old Rouse was abandoned when the Colorado Fuel and Iron Company discovered immense amounts of underground water in the mines during the spring of 1890. Through subterranean channels, the volume increased beyond the handling capacity of the pumps. Tracks, tools and machinery were removed. After abandonment no attention was paid to the tunnels and they caved in at several locations, choking up the underground waterway to such an extent that a great stream of water broke through the surface one mile above Old Rouse in an old dry arroyo. When this dry run was transformed to a large river, enterprising settlers took out ditches until all of the water was appropriated.

On the night before the removal of Old Rouse began, a wake was held over the soon-to-be-abandoned town. Actually it was a ball, not a wake, and a very festive occasion. On March 14, 1900, the *Denver Times* reported that a crew of men under contractor W. R. Davidson began removal of the houses. The company offered a free lot in the company town to those who would move. Removal of the house to the lot could be financed through the company with payments made in monthly installments. At this rate building lots in the new town were given away like kisses at a wedding.

By 1902 the current of life was well established at the new location. It was an ordinary company town. John T. Breen and M. T. Frennan were in charge of running the community for the Colorado Fuel and Iron Company. In all there were about 125 homes, built in the form of a triangle. Over half of them were owned by the miners. The houses extended back from the mouth of the canyon while plateaus and dikes rose behind the town.

Among the 900 or so who lived at Rouse most were foreign born. Yet surprisingly the number of English speaking people was greater than that of the average coal camp. By October of 1901 about 216 men were employed at the mine. A company operated boardinghouse sheltered the single men and was locally famous for its food. It could accommodate 50 workers. In common with many communities in southern Colorado the town had a department store of the Colorado Supply Company. This one was managed by W. L. Patcher of Crested Butte.

The C.F.&I. kept a physician, Dr. W. S. Chapman, in residence at Rouse. He had charge of health measures for the towns of Rouse and Hegron. During the long winter evenings he lectured on health. He also had charge of a free reading room with 20 standard periodicals. Water for the town came from two sources. There were several wells and springs in the canyon. Later in the season when the wells were dry, Rouse got its water from a large storage tank on the hill.

Rouse boasted of its school with all of the enthusiasm that most towns reserved for their saloons. The Rouse school, called Osgood Hall, was the finest in the county. It was moved from Old Rouse on August 29, 1900, and was ready in the new town when the youngsters returned in September. Rouse boasted of having one of the few kindergartens in

Camp and Plant Magazine, from the Western History Collection, Denver Public Library
A view of Rouse, southwest of Walsenburg

Collection of Robert L. Brown
The ruins of Rouse still dot this beautiful meadow

Huerfano county; 50 pupils studied with Miss Julia Mery-wether. In all, 116 students were enrolled at Osgood Hall. At night, when some schools were vacant, a night school was in operation. Here adults could study parliamentary law, selective reading, debating and discussion, infantry drill, athletics and games. Osgood Hall was also used for theatrical purposes and could be fitted out as a complete opera house. A library of 100 volumes was housed at the school. Two boys' clubs, the Rouse and the Huerfano, regularly met there. There were sewing classes, art exhibits, and pedogogical discussions held at mothers' meetings. When nearby Pictou decided to erect a school, it was patterned after the Osgood facility at Rouse.

For a community that took such a pride in its educational opportunities, it somehow seemed appropriate when, in 1953, Alberta Micek of the Dand School at Rouse won the Colorado-Wyoming spelling bee. She went on to represent both states in the National Spelling Bee at Washington, D.C. It would seem that the little red schoolhouse was still doing a big job.

By December of 1900 the mines around New Rouse were taking out 900 tons of coal per day. Three coal formations were tapped at Rouse. They were the Walsen and Cameron veins and the Robinson seam. In general these mines were more free of underground water, requiring only two pumps with a fifty gallon per minute capacity. The "Room and Pillar" was the plan of mining used here. Up on the surface a Victor boxcar loader or shovel at the tipple did the work of seven men. Throughout much of its life Rouse suffered from a manpower shortage.

The mine and the railroad shared offices in the same building. Early Indians referred to the railroad as "plenty wagon, no horse." When the Denver and Rio Grande extended its tracks into Rouse it built a station called Santa Clara. Here two crews were required for service. The decline of Rouse was due to the same factors that killed other coal camps like Pictou or Primero. Almost nothing remains of the town today.

Rouse was located 187 miles south of Denver, 67 miles south of Pueblo and 10 miles south of Walsenburg. Drive south out of the latter town for about 9 miles on U.S. Highway 85-87. At this writing a small black and white sign on the west side of the highway marks the turnoff to Rouse and Pryor. Turn west at this point and drive through Pryor. Where the road forks keep left past the abandoned brick church on the hill above the road. Go along this road for about ¼ mile. Hidden in the grass and extending across the creek, the empty foundations of Rouse are all around you.

48.

RUSSELL

FROM EARLY RECORDS, dating far back into the period of the Spanish occupation of Southern Colorado, limited numbers of itinerant persons seemed always to be in motion getting from one side of the Sangre de Cristo (Blood of Christ) Range of mountains to the other. Although several additional crossings existed, Sangre de Cristo Pass was an early favorite. For one thing, its crest was only 9,459 feet above sea level. The original road from the east went up South Oak Creek to the west of the presently designated North La Veta Pass. On the western descent, the original grade was pretty generally the same as is now followed by U.S. Highway No. 160, but not identically.

In Costilla County, nearly at the bottom of the western side of the old pass, the small community of Sangre de Cristo came into being in the 1880s. Over the years, mining played only an incidental part in its life. Small quantities of silver, gold and copper were reported but little was done about them. When George Crofutt visited the town he mentioned a number of undeveloped mining claims. For a time, the Colorado Coal and Iron Company, operated some mines here and maintained an interest in the town.

From a physical standpoint, the town extended for a distance of about one mile, and was built in the bottom of this rather open valley. Somewhere along the line, the exact date is uncertain now, the name of Sangre de Cristo was dropped and the name of Russell was adopted. Meanwhile just a short

Collection of Fred and Jo Mazzulla
Here was the town of Russell as photographed by O. T. Davis

Collection of Robert L. Brown
Much of Russell still stands

distance to the north, there was another settlement called Placer. Soon it too went through the rigors of a name change and came up with the rather confusing designation of Russell Post Office. At one time there was also a railroad depot called Placer, built at the same place when the Denver and Rio Grande Railroad extended their tracks over the range. It was described as being 10 miles northeast of Fort Garland, really Garland City, and 87 miles from Pueblo. The fare by train was $7.05, or $12.05 for the 207 mile ride from Denver.

As time went on, about 300 people showed up and lived for a time on the southern slopes of Sangre de Cristo Pass. There were several small stores, a sawmill which kept busy turning out ties for the railroad, a school and a church. When the inevitable post office arrived, a Mr. Tate assumed the duties of postmaster. Essentially, Russell was a small farm and ranch town. Sheep and cattle raising were the primary occupations. One resident, Mrs. Jim Jones, said that the peak population was between 800 and 900 in later years.

When Sangre de Cristo Pass fell into disuse after the new La Veta Pass was opened, Russell was left in a rather isolated position. La Veta became a paved pass while Sangre de Cristo withered away. But over the years, La Veta was also a very troublesome crossing to maintain. With its exposed slopes, winter crossings were often treacherous. So another change was made about five years ago, combining the best features of both terrains. The present La Veta Pass is actually North La Veta Pass. Quite apart from names, its western side is nearly identical, as we noted previously, with the old Sangre de Cristo Pass.

In the meantime, the town of Russell had died, and is now one of the few ghost towns having a paved highway that runs right through its location. To see its remaining schoolhouse, empty homes and corrals, drive west on U.S. Highway No. 160 out of Walsenburg, over the pass and toward Fort Garland. The remains of Russell are on the right or north side of the road, about 15 miles east of Fort Garland.

49.

SEGUNDO

FOR NEARLY AS FAR BACK as most residents of the Purgatoire Valley can remember, there have been houses at the mouth of Smith Canyon. In common with Primero, Segundo had two parts. The older section, called Varros, was a Spanish town and grew up around the nucleus of cabins clustered at the entrance to Smith Canyon. Varros was on the north side of the river and just over a quarter of a mile below the later town which was called Segundo. It contained a number of irregular, unpainted adobe structures, yellow frame buildings with high false fronts and a square church with an unfinished belfry. Unlike its more recent neighbor which would absorb it, Varros was neither owned nor controlled by the Colorado Fuel and Iron Company. The elevation here is 6,600 feet above sea level.

First known as Humoso, then as Segundo Ovens, the other half of the town dates from a 1901 coal bed development by the Colorado Fuel and Iron Company. Its location was on the south side of the river and slightly farther west on higher but quite level ground. Construction began in March of 1901 and had been largely completed by 1903. In all, there were about 145 company type houses built here. Down beside the river, all of the 800 coke ovens were in operation by January of 1903. The roundhouse of the Colorado and Wyoming Railroad and the sooty washers covered the remaining space between the mountains and the river. By June of 1901 the railroad had been completed through Segundo and up

Smith Canyon to the Primero Mine. Two passenger trains east and two headed west served Segundo seven days each week.

Tests demonstrated that coal from the Primero Mine was excellent for coking. Following its acquisition of these rich beds, the officials of the C.F.&I. decided to erect washers and coke ovens as near to the Primero as possible. The determining factor in selecting a site was availability of water. Following a series of tests and inspections, the Segundo site was selected, the beehive type coke ovens and the two washers were put up and placed in operation. Each oven was 13 feet in diameter. They were arranged in four double rows, 200 to a row, extending east from the washers and parallel to the river. Their capacity was about 1,500 tons of coke a day. The entire product of the ovens was sold to smelters in Pueblo, Denver, Arizona, New Mexico and Old Mexico. Each of the two washers had a capacity of 1,200 tons each ten hours.

By March of 1903 there were 427 men employed at Segundo. Of this group 347 were employed on the ovens, 60 on the two washers, and 21 on general construction. Roughly half of the men were of Italian extraction. Mexicans, Austrians, and Americans made up the other 50 percent. Including families, the overall population for Segundo was estimated at 1,500 people.

The Mountain Telegraph Company and Western Union occupied a joint office facility at Segundo. As a further stimulus to communication, the Colorado Telephone Company furnished Trinidad local and long distance connections. The switchboard was in the Colorado Supply Company store. Segundo's post office was housed in this same building. Four mails were received and sent out each day. In 1903, there were 20 phone subscribers at Segundo. At the Colorado and Wyoming station the Wells, Fargo Express Company maintained an office.

In the early days one overly precise writer noted that Segundo was located in the southwestern portion of Las Ani-

Camp and Plant Magazine, from the Western History Collection, Denver Public Library
Looking northwest across the town of Segundo

Collection of Robert L. Brown
The present town of Segundo is across the North Fork of the Purgatoire River from
the original site. The railroad bridge seems to be in the same
location; a few trees mark the sites of former homes.

mas County, seventeen and fifty-six hundredths miles west of Trinidad. Many of today's oil company maps show it at this location, on State Highway No. 12, between Valdez and Weston. Today's Segundo, however, is no ghost town and is not the original community. The present town is on the north side of the river. The old Segundo, a true ghost town, was across the river and slightly east. When you reach present-day Segundo, go to any high point in the town and look off to the south. The scars of streets and empty foundations that you see across the river are those of Segundo. East of town, at Valdez, a bridge crosses the river and provides access to the old townsite.

50.

SHAVANO

SHAVANO, THE TOWN, kited its name from a coincidental location at the western base of a great 14,225-foot-high peak that has inspired several ancient legends with origins that are lost in the dim past. All involve the fabled Angel of Shavano, a formation of snow that becomes visible on the peak's eastern side late in the spring and early each summer. In one of these legends a pair of Ute Indian boys, suitors of a girl named Corntassel, fought a duel to the death for the right to possess her. Mortally wounded, the loser mustered sufficient strength to kill the girl too. Almost immediately a celestially inspired drought laid waste to the land and sent the tribe wandering elsewhere, accepting their misfortune as an omen of tribal disgrace, brought on by the innocent girl's death. Eventually they wandered into the Arkansas Valley. Viewing the snowy apparition, they thought of Corntassel. Inspired with renewed faith, they planted corn. An abundant harvest resulted. Until the coming of the white man, the tribe lived happily beneath the eternal promise of the snow maiden.

A second story also involved a drought, but in this one an Indian princess knelt at the base of the mountain to pray for rain. The Great Spirit accepted her as a personal sacrifice, transferring her form to a snowy image, with arms outstretched and emblazoned on the side of Mt. Shavano. Each year as the snow melts, the arid land below becomes fertile.

Another popular explanation for the formation involves the inevitable drought and a mischievous girl whose unrepentant pranks induced the God Jupiter to change her into a figure of white ice, "Until some mishap or tragedy of other people moves you to tears." Contented with her lot, the girl remained there for centuries, until a drought struck the people who lived in the valley below. Filled with compassion, she began to cry and eventually disintegrated or melted to provide water for the crops. Each summer since that time, she has continued to give life so that others might survive.

High up on the western slope of this mountain, some 11,000 feet above sea level, gold was discovered in 1879. In the beginning, early settlers called their "town" Clifton, but as the months passed support grew for a name change and Shavano became the official designation. By the way, the original Shavano was a war chief of the Uncompahgre Utes. Before the town was actually platted in 1880, there were many streets running off through the trees at odd angles. To attract settlers, free building lots were given away to anyone willing to grade his own 25-foot-long frontage. By August of 1880 there were over 100 persons at Shavano. One source says 110 residents.

Throughout most of its life Shavano was regarded as a part of the Monarch Mining District. If contemporary estimates were at all correct, the original townsite covered some 120 acres, although the *Salida Mountain Mail* said it was only 90 acres with 30 log cabins. Although it was located adjacent to the North Fork of the Arkansas River, the actual source of the town's water supply was Cyclone Creek. Both water and firewood were always free as long as the town lasted. From the snowy slopes above the town, a wooden flume carried additional water down, supplementing the volume available from the creek. From Maysville, a steep toll road was extended up the valley. Before that time Shavano had been receiving its supplies by pack mules. With its completion the pack trains were replaced by wagons. From the Hughes Hotel at Maysville, transients could ride a stagecoach up to Shavano for only 75 cents.

From the standpoint of location, Shavano was in a most fortunate position indeed. Most of its cabins were built among the trees nestled in a dense growth of huge old evergreens that afforded a modicum of protection from wind, weather and snowslides. Within the town, quite a number of business establishments flourished, one real estate agency, an apparent rarity among mining camp ventures, was operated at Shavano by McAleer and Rice Company. At the peak of the boom there were three well-stocked general stores ready to supply a wide variety of merchandise. To meet certain other needs, Charley Wilson operated Shavano's only saloon.

Down through the years, a total of three gold mills were erected. One of these was a huge three storied structure that stood by the edge of the stream. One sawmill managed to accommodate most of the customers for construction materials. Shavano was also the headquarters town for the Miners and Prospectors Union. Within the Monarch Mining District, some 100 men belonged to this federation. George Nichols of Shavano was the president of the union. In point of total time, the crime rate here was remarkably low. If contemporary records were at all correct, there was only one murder and one hanging, both of which involved the same individual. All things considered, Shavano's low incidence of criminal activity was commendable and not too typical when measured by the standards of its time.

In all, Shavano lasted for a mere 5 years with its gold excitement. Then for many years it was deserted. But in 1904 there was a second boom when both silver and lead were discovered nearby. Yet with all these developments Shavano's second lease on life was over in just 3 more years. Taken as a whole, Shavano has been a ghost town for at least the last half century.

The road up to Shavano is no longer difficult. Drive west of Poncha Springs on U.S. Highway No. 50 toward Monarch Pass. Just beyond Maysville, watch for the U.S. Forest

Service sign about the Shavano campground which will appear on the north (right) side of the highway. At this point turn north, following the rough dirt road up the valley. Stay on the main road. At Shavano itself, a Forest Service marker provides a brief history of the old town. Beyond the sign, the ruins of several buildings can be found off among the trees. At this writing one of the old mills is still up, just a short walk to the west of the road. Looming above the valley to the east, the barren slopes of Mt. Shavano still dominate the valley, but the snow-angel formation is around on the eastern side and is not visible from the old town.

Collection of Robert L. Brown
The Snowy Angel of Shavano, with outstretched arms, and Mt. Shavano

Collection of Robert L. Brown
At Shavano, this is one of two cabins that still have their walls and roofs intact

51.

SILVER CREEK

ON THE EASTERN SLOPE of Columbia Mountain, two miles above and south of the town of Lawson, a small mining community called Chinn City or Daileyville sprang to life on March 1, 1884. Named for James Dailey, the settlement was built adjacent to the narrow and shallow Silver Creek, a tributary of Clear Creek. Almost immediately the settlement was renamed Silver Creek. Silver Creek empties into Clear Creek at a point slightly to the east of Lawson.

At various times in the history of the camp, James Dailey acted as a resident manager of the adjacent mining properties. His name was also perpetuated by the Dailey Tunnel, a silver property that went down to a depth of 800 feet. Quite a number of mineral properties were active in the vicinity of the camp. Among them were the Jo Reynolds properties, owned by Diamond Jo Reynolds of Chicago. The O'Connell Tunnel was 1,100 feet long and was cut in laterally to its silver vein. A firm known as Marsh and Company had eight men at work there in 1884, excavating in the O'Connell Tunnel. Another firm, Herrick and Company, excavated the engine chamber where heavy equipment would eventually be installed. When completed, the excavation was sufficiently large enough to accommodate an underground dance. The management proposed this unique celebration in honor of their completed construction schedule. Among others, the entire newspaper staff from the neighboring *Georgetown Miner* was invited to participate in the subsurface festivities. Most of the ores from the O'Connell Tunnel were sent down to Lawson, by wagon for refinement.

The American Sisters Group, better known as the Silver Creek Belt of Mines, contained the Magnet and the Sequel, two of the better properties in this section of Clear Creek County. Both of these mines were on Summit Mountain, now called Saxon Mountain. All of the American Sisters Group was managed by Ernest La Neve Foster. Over the years, these properties produced between 150 and 300 ounces of silver to the ton.

Long before any settlement had been started here, a limited amount of mining activity was being carried on. For example, the Pickwick Lode was worked during 1876-77. Other active mines were the Charter Oak, Anglo Saxon, Federal Lode, Wyandotte, Saxon Extension and Harrington. Although Silver Creek seems never to have been incorporated as a town, there was nevertheless a school with 25 pupils enrolled. Like so many other similar settlements Silver Creek was always a small place. While a fairly large number of miners found employment around Silver Creek, not all of them chose to live there. Consequently no post office was ever established. Throughout the life of the camp, the men and their families always picked up their mail at Lawson.

Inevitably, since the mines here left much to be desired, the life of the town was of rather short duration. With the decline, residents and their families moved away to try their luck at the other favored localities of the moment. At this writing, the trail up to Silver Creek is a rough, but not dangerous, 4-wheel-drive road. Start at Lawson, west of Idaho Springs, barely off to the side of the new Interstate No. 70. Drive to the large red mill beside the South Fork of Clear Creek, at the western edge of Lawson. Take the paved road that leads off to the south and crosses the creek. Immediately after you cross the bridge, turn abruptly left or east and start up the mountain. At the first fork, encountered almost immediately, turn right and continue climbing. In general, stay with the most used trail for about 1½ miles. Where the trail forks again, close to the mine dumps, Silver Creek is there, barely beyond the forks. This road through the town goes on up to some of the mines. Although the only cabins are now to the left of the road as you enter the town, originally there were others over among the timber. A casual search will reveal their foundations.

Going back a few yards to the main trail, if time permits, you might enjoy the rough but very scenic ride over Saxon Mountain. Although this is an easy one as Jeep roads go, caution should be exercised on the ledge section. After crossing the top, this road intersects with a somewhat better trail. A turn to the right will carry you to Magnet Park and a dead-end, overlooking Silver Plume. A left turn will take you past an old and unnamed logging camp that was apparently used to secure lumber, while Freeland and Lamartine were being built. Farther along, the road forks again at Lamartine. One of the two roads will take you out by way of Ute Creek while the other, the left branch, descends to Trail Creek. Both will take you back to Idaho Springs.

Collection of Robert L. Brown
A vista along the ledge road up Saxon Mountain near Silver Creek

Collection of Robert L. Brown
The few remaining cabins of Silver Creek are scattered
throughout the trees, high on a mountainside.

52.

SILVER DALE

HIGH UP ON THE SLOPES of Leavenworth Mountain, roughly
1½ miles south of Georgetown, silver-bearing ores were discovered during the summer of 1864. But little was done
about it, since the technology of that time had not yet revealed a satisfactory method of refining the white metal. By
the middle 1870s, a collocation of cabins had begun to cluster around the junction of Leavenworth and South Clear
creeks. Although it soon acquired a name, it had no shape
or core and as yet no formal streets. Silver Dale was simply
an assemblage of rude log buildings, flung down without
much thought among the far-scattered clumps of timber
near the base of the mountain. There were two towns, Upper
Dale and Lower Dale. In general, most of the abodes were
scattered in the narrow valley of Leavenworth Gulch. This
town was rarely shown on contemporary maps.

Erl Ellis, Denver attorney and founder of the Silver Dale
Club, found that a Mrs. Emma Jane Wallace Whiteside was
the first female resident of the town. Although growth was
slow in the 70s, Silver Dale managed to acquire a post office,
a couple of general stores, and one hotel that was run by a
Mrs. Wentworth. There were stores and boardinghouses at
either end of town. The principal street, incidentally, was
about 4,000 feet long. Although Silver Dale had two grave-
yards at one time, the one belonging to Upper Dale was covered by a mudslide in 1925. In the *Georgetown Miner* for
January 16, 1875, there is a description of an operating school

for the children of the miners at Silver Dale. Known as Colorado School District 7, this institution of learning functioned until its merger with Georgetown in 1893. A toll road connected the two towns.

In a later issue of the *Miner,* one may read about a Silver Dale resident named Jerry Kirthley, a fiddler, who 'twas alleged, "produced good solid left-handed music." On one occasion a roving reporter from the same paper spent Christmas at Silver Dale. His account of the occasion as printed in the next issue leaves room for a bit of reading between the lines.

Christmas left the town with a decidedly successful headache. If the Birthday of Bethlehem's Babe is always to leave behind it such a thumping legacy, I am not sorry that we will not have another occurrance for at least 12 months.

Several mines grew up around the original strikes that had been made on Leavenworth Mountain, and they managed to provide an economic basis for the town's existence. Probably the best of the lot was the Colorado Central Mine, a deep property served by the Marshall Tunnel. Nearby, as the crow flies, were the Robinson and Curtley mines; the Equator, Big Blue and S. J. Tilden. Two colored miners, Thomas Perry and Louis Cowan, leased an open tract on Leavenworth Mountain. Working their property through the Robinson Tunnel, Perry and Cowan, hit a vein of silver 60 feet down and named it the Star Lode. Their mine produced so well that they were able to sub-let its lower level to other miners.

Fate, moving along oblique lines gave Silver Dale its day of infamy. The date was March 19, 1874. It all started when six townsmen named Thompson, Wright, Trapp, McClurg, Mackey and Hammond, entered the architectural abortion that sheltered the local booze juggler. Here they sat down for a "seige with the grape," sprawled among the tobacco fumes and sour athletic odors. Sometime before midnight the party moved to Thompson's cabin where their liquid festivities were resumed and everyone became enchantingly stewed.

Shortly before 1:00 A.M. a dispute developed between two of the principals when George Hammond began an unflattering review of William Mackey's family tree. In frustration, Mackey threw off his coat and took a swing at Hammond. The latter rose unsteadily from his chair and began dancing about his opponent like a cannibal around a missionary. The slightly bibulous but enthusiastic audience said that it really was a good fight and that this formal part lasted for about seven minutes.

Mackey, while getting the worst of it on the floor, implored the spectators to take Hammond off him. Yowling like a great and pestiferous tomcat, Hammond said he would get up only when Mackey admitted that he had had enough. When Mackey threatened to kill his opponent, Hammond offered to stop if the other man would "call it square." Though his chances were little better than those of a martyr among Roman lions, Mackey vowed that he would suffer death first, somehow rolled out from under his oppressor, got up and lurched out of the door.

Few obstacles could check the pent up fury of the alcoholic Mackey. In 15-20 minutes he was back; armed with a revolver. Thompson, Wright, Trapp, McClurg, and Hammond locked both the doors and the windows. Mackey circled the cabin, baying like a hound with the rabies. When he threatened to shoot the lock off the door, Hammond made an exit through a window. The effects of his recent participation in the National Wine Week festivities were still with him and Hammond clumsily stumbled over a pile of wood, stacked beneath his point of departure.

Three shots were fired. Subsequent testimony indicated that Mackey fired the first and third shot while Hammond got off the second one. When the men in the cabin staggered out, they found Mackey writhing on the ground. He was carried in and placed on Thompson's bunk. Twenty-five

Collection of Francis and Freda Rizzari
Silver Dale, west of Georgetown

Collection of Robert L. Brown
The Green Lake-Guanella Pass road now passes the old site of Silver Dale

minutes later he was dead. Almost immediately after the shooting, the killer started for Georgetown. He surrendered himself when the sheriff opened his doors the following morning. All of the witnesses were present at the inquest, conducted by Charles R. Fish, justice of the peace. Mackey, it seems, died from a gunshot wound adroitly placed in his bowels. In his confession, George Hammond admitted that he had shot Mackey, "above where I aimed." Justice Fish ruled that the homicide was justified and that Hammond had acted in self defense. Georgetown's coroner sustained the decision. Hammond was released and at once returned to his home in Silver Dale.

In the *Georgetown Miner* for March 20, 1876, an account of the foregoing tragedy appeared. Immediately beside it on the same page, too close for coincidence, was a big-headline plea from the Female Temperance Society of Clear Creek County. Its oversize title was called, *An Earnest Plea To The Liquor Sellers of Georgetown by the Ladies.* A hastily called meeting of this organization had formed a committee to appeal to the liquor sellers. Some quotes from the article follow: "Drunkards are multiplied by the number of liquor sellers in town. Close up and make a living for your families in some legitimate way." "Stop making sober men drunkards before you fall victims of your own immoral traffic." "What profit will you have if you have become a drunkard?" "Seven out of ten liquor sellers become drunkards."

Life at Silver Dale continued on until the repeal of the Sherman Silver Purchase Act came out of Washington's legislative sausage machine in 1893. At that time, in common with so many other silver camps, the town began dying by stages. Today, except for a few headstones below the road, nothing remains at the site. To get there, take the Green Lake-Guanella Pass road up out of Georgetown. When you have driven 1½ miles, you are at the former location of Silver Dale.

53.

SPRINGDALE

EDGAR SMITH HAD WALKED briskly through the scattered evergreen forest that lined both banks of Jim Creek for most of an afternoon. At dusk he came to a meadow above the waters and made his camp. Close by, a spring gushed from the earth. Smith lay on his belly and drank; the water had a strange, earthy, mineralized taste. Stumbling back down to the creek, he rinsed out his mouth and drank deeply of "those waters which had the pure and more familiar taste of melted snows."

Although old records reveal that the earliest explorers who visited this valley were also attracted by the mineral springs, it remained for Smith to do something about them. In some accounts, the initial C or E appears before his first name. He was a native of upper New York state. From the fact that he found these springs in a dale, he contrived the name of Springdale, a name that was original enough to last. In content, the springs contained soda, sulphur and iron. From the standpoint of temperature, there were both hot and cold waters. At that time they were considered to have a valuable medicinal content.

Smith, who had traveled in Europe prior to coming west, saw a resemblance between these springs and some others he had seen in Germany. He made a number of improvements and organized an advertising campaign to promote Springdale and its healing waters as a summer resort. Up on the hill, at the top of the gulch, another mineral spring was found. It was named for its discoverer and became Peabody's Mineral Springs. Back down the hill in Left Hand Canyon, the Seltzer House Hotel was built. Close at hand, they also put up somewhere between eight and ten small family cottages for their patrons. A bottling plant was set up near the springs. The healing waters were bottled up and enjoyed a rather wide sale in various parts of the United States.

Although Springdale experienced its greatest fame as a health resort after 1880, it had also gone through a previous existence as a not-very-successful mining camp. In 1874, mines that produced telluride ores were discovered on the hillsides above James (Jim) Creek, actually a branch of Left Hand Creek. An early account describes the settlement as being seven miles north and four miles west of Boulder at an elevation of 8,580 feet above sea level. A village post office was established and J. V. Sylvant, the local assayer, assumed the duties of postmaster. A combination general store and saloon was operated by E. Holzinger and Company. In later years, health faddists who preferred to imbibe of the healing waters, referred to Holzinger's Saloon as "the garbage chute."

Among the mining properties worked at Springdale were the Ellen, Golden Age, Gladiator, Longfellow, King William, Glasgow, Grand Central, Ohio, Rip Van Dam, Lillie of the West, Big Blossom, Louie, Wano and the Copper Blush. Springdale was listed in the Colorado Business Directory for the first time in 1877. Later, of course, a fine carriage road was hacked out of the hillsides above the creek and stagecoaches from Boulder served the camp. Prior to 1880, there had been about three hundred people at Springdale. After it became a health resort and acquired a reputation, for some reason the population dwindled. Only forty permanent residents were there in 1890. By 1893, only ten still held out. Their faith was justified when forty-five people had settled there by 1898. In 1900 there were one hundred and fifty there and the same total showed up again for 1904.

Springdale as it looked before the 1894 flood

The empty site of Springdale, showing James Creek at the left of the highway

Actually, Springdale itself was wiped out when it was caught by the Jim Creek flood of 1894. Most of the buildings that were close to the creek were lost. More than any other single factor, the flood accounts for the decline of Springdale. Although the mines played out, the springs did not dry up.

To see what remains of Springdale, drive straight north out of Boulder for fifteen miles on State Highway 7. At the point where Left Hand Creek intersects with the highway from the west, turn left up the canyon toward Ward. At the first place where a paved road leaves the highway to the right, about five miles up, turn and go toward Jamestown for about two miles. A white sign on the left side of the road marks the site of Springdale. A few houses stand below the sign. Actually, the original town was about a quarter of a mile beyond this sign, below the highway to the left, along the creek. A comparison of the site with the accompanying photographs will reveal the previous location. On the hillsides, there are still some buildings which escaped the flood. However, since most of the original Springdale was built in the bottom of the valley along the bed of the creek, not even the old foundations remain.

54.

SUNSET

FAR TOO MANY of our concepts about life in the west have stemmed from the commercially marketable fantasies of Madison Avenue or Hollywood. Such places as Dodge City, Leadville, or Deadwood were rare exceptions that should be noted as such. In actual fact, most western towns were surprisingly quiet and orderly places in which to live. Sunset was one of these.

In its earliest existence, a limited amount of mining in Four Mile Canyon attracted enough people to warrant the establishment of a village post office there in 1884. All mail was routed up from Boulder. The Honorable John L. Routt, last Territorial Governor and first Governor of the new State of Colorado, invested heavily in the Free Coinage Mine at Sunset. Another good property was called the Poor Woman, and the Scandia Mine was situated on a hillside above the town.

As towns go, Sunset was always a small place. There was just one hotel, the Columbine. Three general merchandise stores were run by Adolph Alpert, William La Shell, and the Dalton and Sullivan Company respectively. W. T. Linticum opened a meat and provisions store that lasted for many years. The town was fortunate in that it was built on the already existing line of the Greeley, Salt Lake and Pacific Railroad.

A series of population statistics published in the Colorado Business Directory at various times gives us some indication of the size of Sunset. In 1890 its records showed forty residents in the town. By 1894 this number had jumped up to 175. There were still 175 people there again in 1897. Shortly after the turn of the century, in 1901, Sunset had fallen back to a population of 75. For 1903 the same total was again reported. By 1921, the last year for which figures were recorded, the total had dropped to a mere handful—just 30 people. These figures would tend to substantiate an estimate found elsewhere which stated that Sunset's period of optimum development was in the 1890s. After that, the peak was passed.

Sunset derived immense benefits from the railroad that ran through the town. Three different names appear in this connection. Actually, all three refer to the same railroad right-of-way under three different incorporations. The heyday of railroad sight-seeing occurred during the mining boom at Sunset. In pre-automobile days, loop excursions transported large numbers of sightseers up Four Mile Canyon, around the hills and into most of the better known mining communities. The Greeley, Salt Lake and Pacific which served Sunset was never able to pay its own way. The Union Pacific tried its hand at operating the road but could not show a profit. Torrential rains fell on May 30, 1894, inundating the mountains and canyons west of Boulder. In the freshet that followed, the tracks were washed away. When faced by the prospect of more red ink, the Union Pacific threw up its hands and got out.

It was nearly inevitable that others should try where the Union Pacific had failed. Two Pennsylvanians, W. J. Culbertson and Colonel Sam Dick, bought and regraded the old right-of-way. By 1897 they were at work building their Colorado and Northwestern Railway. Actually, this was a mining railroad. In addition to Culbertson and Dick, there were five others who invested in the venture. Between them, these seven men owned all of the stock. Two different sets of dates have been given for the arrival of the rails in Sunset. One says they reached Sunset in that same year, 1897.

Courtesy Library, State Historical Society of Colorado
An early photograph of Sunset showing the railroad trestle
leading to the town at the right.

Collection of Robert L. Brown
This contemporary view of Sunset was made from the road to Mt. Alto Park

Another article insists they did not get there until January of 1898. In any event, this highly scenic route was soon dubbed the "Switzerland Trail' or the "Whiplash Route." For many years thereafter, the spruced up old Columbine Hotel put its best foot forward and accommodated fifty persons at a time for meals while the train ran. For the owners, these tourists became a veritable gold mine above ground. By the following July, tracks had been extended into Ward.

In general, the original grades have now become automobile roads. From Boulder, the tracks went up Boulder Canyon to Four Mile Canyon. Along the way, trains passed through Crisman, Salina, and Wall Street before pulling into Sunset. Here the road divided. A right fork went up over the hill to Mt. Alto, with its handsome fountain, hotel, picnic ground, and dance hall. From this point the tracks went on to Ward. On the other, or left, branch from Sunset the tracks climbed up along the steep face of Sugarloaf Mountain to the town of Sugarloaf. Next, the tracks were built to the west along a ridge past Glacier Lake before dropping down into Cardinal. The tracks reached Eldora in 1904 and first saw service on New Year's Day of 1905.

After the company went into receivership in March of 1909, a reorganization was effected as the Denver, Boulder, and Western Railway. Following another cloudburst in 1919, the whole thing was abandoned. A few buildings still mark the site of Sunset but much of the town is gone now. The site is five miles west and one mile south of Gold Hill. To get there, take State Highway No. 119 west into Boulder Canyon for about a mile. At the Gold Hill sign, turn north (right) and drive through Crisman to Salina. At this point the road divides. Keep left through Wall Street to Sunset. Except in winter, both of the original railroad grades out of town are passable and offer some rather pretty vistas of the surrounding countryside.

55.

SWANDYKE

HIGH UP ON THE Middle Fork of the Swan River, not far below Wise Mountain and the Continental Divide, a great sulphide belt lay waiting to be tapped. This belt was generally considered to be the same one which crosses Colorado and the Blue River country from northeast to southwest. At Swandyke, it was thought to be particularly close to the surface and to have oxidized, freeing a large proportion of the gold. From the crest of the great divide, melting snows sent waters down to the Platte River and to the Atlantic Ocean. Just a few feet away, from the opposite side of the same range, the spring run-off eventually reached the Pacific. In this high and rarefied atmosphere, the obscure and short-lived community of Swandyke was established.

Although most Colorado mining districts were rather small, the Swandyke mining district embraced most of the country around the headwaters of the North, Middle, and South forks of the Swan River. Here, rich gold ore was found just before the turn of the century. Large veins of sulphide and partly oxidized minerals were found in abundance. All carried gold that was valued from $5 to $25 to the ton. Some of the mines, like the Brilent, were on the mountainsides above the town, more than 13,000 feet high.

In the town itself, there was a good hotel, with accommodations for 75 people, a well-supplied general store, a blacksmith shop, a sawmill, and many fine single-family dwellings, primarily log cabins. Some 200 men and their families established themselves in the district. Shortly after the town had started to grow, a post office was authorized and formally established on April 12, 1899. Mr. S. Stridiron was appointed to serve as the first postmaster. A reference in the State Historical Society of Colorado noted that special services were to be supplied from Wapiti. Apparently these services were not very special, because other arrangements were soon made to get mail delivered from Jefferson. On November 14, 1899, the whole thing was discontinued.

When one looks back at the formidable array of mining properties being worked in the Swandyke District, the brief life span of the town is difficult to understand. The Carrie group of mines had both free milling and concentrating ores, developed by a long tunnel. In addition, the group owned and operated its own stamp mill. Another property, the Pompeii, worked a large vein of partly oxidized ore and also had its own stamp mill. The Swandyke Gold Mining and Milling Company started out with eight properties, which were soon expanded to an even dozen. These were operated through the summer of 1900, with plans to continue work through the winter. Their claims showed average assays of from $70 to $80 in gold. Other properties were named the Tyler, 3 Kings, Uncle Sam, Gibbs, and Potter.

Plans were made to erect a new 10-stamp "custom" ore mill in the Swandyke district. Among the promoters there was a strong belief that extensive veins of sulphides were, practically speaking, not to be exhausted by deep mining. One ore claim, a trench run for purposes of discovery, opened a large vein barely three feet below the surface. In it they found an 18 inch streak of galena that carried about $90 to the ton. Another claim had a single 50 foot shaft in an oxidized ore formation that carried from one to five ounces of gold to the ton. A four foot body of lead was unearthed in one of the mines which showed a value of $27 in gold, $8.30 in silver, 50 percent lead and 4 percent copper to the ton. In still another, a streak of gold-bearing quartz showed par-

ticles of gold visible to the naked eye. Subsequent assays
yielded $1,855 to the ton, while the entire body of ore was of
shipping value.

In a publication of that day, *The Great Sulphide Belt and
Swandyke District,* R. G. Dill speculated that the opportunities here were enough to sustain a large population for many
years. He also described the abundant timber, available in
every direction, and an inexhaustible water supply. There
was a further suggestion that the topography of the gulches
afforded rare opportunities for electric power plants. Finally,
he recommended Swandyke as "A summer resort above praise.
Clear air, warm days, cool nights, and numberless opportunities for sylvan sports afforded a combination that appeals
strongly to those who go to the mountains for rest and recu-
peration of lost energies."

Geologically, Swandyke was built in a vast natural amphi-
theatre of somewhat irregular proportions. On every side,
evidences of volcanic activity and mineralization may still
be seen. Missouri Hill is the northernmost of the enclosing
walls of the basin on the western side. To the south are Bull
Mountain, Buck Hill, Sheep Mountain, Alpine Mountain and
Wise Mountain, which forms the northern rim of the basin
before extending down to Farncomb Hill and Lincoln City
on the other side of the range. Most of the mining development here was by tunnel, as the hills were very steep. The
dip of the veins was easily determined, minimizing the usual
risks in tunneling propositions.

An early transportation prospectus noted that there were
two good wagon roads, built by the people themselves, into
the town from either Breckenridge or Jefferson Station.
From this latter point, the nearest railroad station, the distance to Denver was a mere 75 miles on the Colorado and
Southern Railroad. A stagecoach from Jefferson connected
with the train that left Denver at 8:15 A.M. For many years,
a stagecoach left Jefferson at 2:00 P.M., arriving in Swandyke at 6:00 P.M., all in the same day's trip from Denver.

Incidentally, the morning train from Leadville to Denver also made connections with the stage at Jefferson. Georgia Pass, now a wild 4-wheel-drive road on its western side, crossed the Continental Divide from the head of Michigan Creek. From its 11,598 foot crest, it descended down the south fork of the Swan River, providing easy access to Swandyke.

Although Swandyke was often deserted in winter miners sometimes chose to remain and work their claims during the cold months. The winter of 1898-99 was such an occasion. On September 15, the first snow fell. By October the higher peaks were covered. Many of the residents used snowshoes for going to work and for traveling around the town. On November 27, the snow started falling. At 9:00 A.M. on the 28th it was 5 feet deep on the level in Swandyke. According to those who spent the winter there, additional snow fell every day until February 20th. With such quantities of white drifts hanging on the sheer mountainsides, avalanches began to run. Some of them destroyed buildings in the town. Residents rolled up their bedding, put on their snowshoes and headed for Breckenridge.

Additional snows brought added hardships for Breckenridge. No trains were able to reach the town for 94 days. Drifts of snow on the flats reached a depth of 20 feet. Supplies in the stores were inadequate for the 150 people in the town. Dairy cows were slaughtered for food. After 15 days of exhausting labor, the Boreas Pass road to Como was opened and food supplies were brought in. But it was June before the residents of Swandyke were able to return to their town on snowshoes. Upon arrival they discovered that an avalanche had carried their mill from one side of the mountain, across a deep gulch, leaving the rubble on the opposite mountainside.

The 17 mile wagon road over Georgia Pass was shoveled out across the divide to Jefferson, using a work crew of nearly 100 men. They reached Jefferson the first day of July. On July 4 the first stagecoach crossed the pass from South Park

Swandyke, high in the mountains of Summit County

Completely abandoned in its lofty setting, here was Swandyke in 1967·

to Swandyke, threading its way between 20 foot high snow-banks on both sides of the road. Six horses were used to get the vehicle through.

Despite all the glowing prospects, the life of Swandyke was short. It was all over in just a few years. For one thing, transportation was difficult, and the location, as just described, was pretty remote. For another, mining in Colorado had started to decline after the turn of the century, except for a few favored localities like Creede or Cripple Creek. Actually, Cripple Creek, the second greatest gold camp the world has ever known, provided pretty tough competition for the smaller camps such as Swandyke. The history of Colorado for this period is replete with references to miners leaving this place or that to try their luck at Cripple Creek.

If you continue on up the rutted trail for a mile or so, you will arrive at another small settlement known as Upper Swandyke. Here the road ends. Several cabins and one old water wheel are still to be seen.

Whether you decide to see Swandyke from Georgia Pass or from the other side, you are in for some 4-wheel-drive travel, or a long hike. It is somewhat easier to find from the western slope. From Frisco, take Colorado State Highway No. 9 south toward Breckenridge. Turn left at the point where a dirt road branches east (left) up the Swan River to Tiger. Beyond Tiger, where the road forks, go straight ahead on the right branch to the middle fork of the Swan River at the next fork of the trail. If you turn right and reach the site of Parkville, turn around and go back to the fork. The rocky trail to Swandyke is rather steep but not difficult in a 4-wheel-drive vehicle. Three buildings on the left side of the trail, set among extensive evidence of mining activity, are all that remain of Swandyke. Some other foundations may be found among the trees. This is a beautiful location, well worth taking a few extra moments to hike around and enjoy the scenery.

56.

TABASCO

TABASCO WAS A NEW community in 1901. Like so many of its neighboring coal mining towns, it was owned by the Colorado Fuel and Iron Company. Located just a mile from Berwind in Road Canyon, and some 17 miles northwest of Trinidad, Tabasco had a somewhat unusual town plat. It was separated into two residential districts, about ¾ mile apart. Between them stood C.F.&I. mine No. 34, source of the town's support.

Private residences at Tabasco were of the cottage type, a style of house much preferred by coal mine operators and town builders. Here the capacity of the houses varied. The smallest structures had four rooms while the bigger ones contained six. Diversity of design, it was felt, relieved the appearance of monotony so common in turn-of-the-century coal camps. Most had plastered walls inside. Exterior colors varied considerably with the whim of the occupants.

Tabasco's population was quite diverse. Here one could find a mixture of Italians, Mexicans, Austrians, Scotsmen, and Americans. Generally speaking, the town's population hovered around 1,500. Of this group 485 men were employed at the mine or in the other C.F.&I. agencies that flourished in the town.

Both a coke oven and a coal washing plant were located at Tabasco. The washer had a peak capacity of 1,200 tons of coal daily. The ovens have been variously referred to as C.F.&I. "H" type and as "bee hive" ovens. Electricity was used to haul the loaded coal cars from the mouth of the mine to the washer and tipple. Gravity alone ran the cars to the coke ovens. No motor power was required for discharging the slack into the Loric cars.

As in most company towns, the Colorado Supply Company operated the only store. James McGavey was the manager of this general store type of operation. For the company, James Cameron was the superintendent of the mine. Tabasco had two physicians, both "company" doctors. Dr. A. L. Trout was a surgeon and was assigned to both Tabasco and to neighboring Berwind. Dr. George D. Andrews was a general practitioner assigned to look after the health of Tabasco.

In 1904 the Colorado and Southeastern Railroad extended its tracks westward through Ludlow, then southwest through Road Canyon and on to Berwind and Tabasco. This line was in place until 1952. Curiously, the Colorado and Southeastern had no passenger service. It was strictly a utilitarian coal-hauling railroad. Incidentally, some railroad maps show a different spelling for Tabasco. In these instances it has appeared as Tobasca.

Since Tabasco and Berwind were just a mile apart, a single school facility was shared by both towns. Fortunately for these towns, land was found at a point midway between them and the school was erected there. Tabasco, like Berwind, had its own separate postal facility.

When coal mining became uneconomical the mine began to curtail production, people moved elsewhere, the railroad stopped operating and the post office closed down. To see Tabasco now, drive south from Walsenburg on Interstate 25 or on the older U.S. 85-87 highway that parallels the 4-lane interstate route. At the Ludlow exit, turn west to the Ludlow massacre site and monument. Here the road forks with one branch going on west to Hastings and Delagua while the other follows the railroad grade off to the southwest. Stay with the railroad grade through the ghost town

Tabasco, the coal camp in Road Canyon, during its heyday

Here is Tabasco as it looked in 1969

of Ludlow. Just beyond the old school, the road bends to the right and then left again. Just beyond this point a right turn takes you through a narrow tunnel beneath the railroad tracks. You are now in Road Canyon. The first settlement that you enter is Tabasco, less than a mile from the railroad tracks. Tabasco is now occupied by a number of cattle pens scattered among its few remaining buildings.

57.

TERCIO

OF ALL THE COAL mining camps scattered throughout southern Colorado Tercio probably had the most picturesque location. On three sides the site is cradled by low lying, thickly-wooded hills. To the north the Sangre de Cristos push skyward in misty rows of cracked escarpments. In terms of age, Tercio is the youngest of the Colorado Fuel and Iron Company towns. In the beginning it was called Torres, later it was Rincon, and finally Tercio as it took its place among the numerical sequence of towns. In Spanish, Primero, Segundo and Tercio mean first, second, and third; presumably ranging west in order from Trinidad.

In common with its neighboring camps, Tercio was a part of the Maxwell Grant, one of the original Spanish land cessions. Although some squatters managed to wrest homestead land from the owners, almost none of the natural resources were exploited prior to 1900. Tercio dates from November of 1901. Because Tercio was some distance away from its sister towns, a scant 6 miles north of the New Mexico border, little time was lost in extending the tracks of the Colorado and Wyoming Railroad through the Purgatoire River Valley to the camp. During its best years two daily passenger trains connected Tercio with the outside world. In view of the connections existing between the parent companies, it was inevitable that a branch store of the Colorado Supply Company would be opened at Tercio. In this case the structure was a rather pretentious one, built of native stone, and described by the residents of the town as, "artistic." Inside, in addition to the usual array of goods and nostrums, one could find the local post office.

In addition to the river, numerous natural springs contributed to the water supply that was fed into the numerous single family dwellings that housed the wives and children of the miners. Like miners elsewhere, those who toiled here spent their time in digging, blasting, housekeeping, and waiting for something to happen.

During the peak years of mining, six openings were worked on coal veins that varied in thickness from four to twelve feet. Daily output was about four hundred tons before the tipple and screens were completed. Near the camp the best openings were called simply numbers One and Two North and One and Two South. The rich Vega mine was situated about 1½ miles south of the camp. Coal from the Vega was moved to the tipple by a steam powered conveyor. For most of the other mines, inclined planes were used. Loaded cars coming down pulled the empties back up. Both the washer and the tipple were situated at a narrow point in the canyon adjacent to the entrance to the camp.

One of the most impressive sights at Tercio could be seen at the eastern edge of town. Here several rows of native stone coke ovens extended for ¾ of a mile. As shown in the accompanying photograph, the neat rows of cottages were off to the south of the coke ovens. Economic factors that brought about the decline of Southern Colorado's coal camps were also responsible for depopulating Tercio. Here, the decline was hastened somewhat by the cost of those long hauls to market. At this writing only empty foundations, the coke ovens, and a large ranch remain at the former site of Tercio.

To visit Tercio drive west from Trinidad on Colorado State Highway No. 12. Beyond Weston the character of the Purgatoire Valley changes, becoming lush with green foliage, while in the background the massive summits of the Sangre

Camp and Plant Magazine, from the Western History Collection, Denver Public Library
View of Tercio looking south. Washer, coke ovens, and Colorado and Wyoming
Railroad tracks are in the foreground, cottages are visible in the distance.

Collection of Robert L. Brown
The nearly empty site of Tercio in 1962

de Cristo Range rise sheer from the valley floor. From Weston to Stonewall, the road winds along through a whole series of very pleasant scenic vistas. In the center of the town of Stonewall, turn south (left) onto a dirt road. Tercio is just 9 miles down this road.

58.

TIGER

VIEWED IN RETROSPECT, the life span of Tiger extended across far more years than that of most of its contemporaries. In a historical sense, Tiger may be dated from 1864. At the opposite end of the time spectrum, it lasted as a mining camp until 1930.* In that earlier day, prospectors from Gregory Gulch migrated into South Park and ultimately crossed the range to the headwaters of the Blue River. One of the first settlements to be established during that early period was Breckenridge. With this town as a base of operations, mining men began a systematic scouring of the nearby peaks and valleys. Good strikes were made in French Gulch and in its neighboring declivity currently known as Barney Ford Gulch.

Then in 1864 D. W. Willey, George Reed and Corydon Smith started up the Swan River on a prospecting trip. In the course of their explorations they uncovered the great Tiger lode. Later that same year, Reed and Willey returned to the valley in company with Jacob Perry, Thomas Cleary and George Packard. After a rather brief search they discovered the Tiger Extension. Both of these finds were made well before the Congress had legislated on the subject of mining claims.

With two great producers already in evidence, an im-

---

*Actually the first people here lived a few hundred feet down the river and called their town Swan City. There was a separate Swan City post office until 1880. The name of Tiger was adopted later.

patient crowd surged up the valley and began the age-old process of setting up a tent city which quickly gave way to a log cabin type of town, with the structures huddled together to assure protection from marauding bands of Utes. In this as in so many other cases, the men chose to call their town after the most prominent mines. Thus Tiger came into being. Sometimes, from the consequence of its location on the river, the men called it "Tiger on the Swan."

Quite apart from the town's actual proximity to the Swan, Tiger actually became a part of the nearby Snake River Mining District, one of the earliest of many such districts that subsequently existed in Summit County. Within a few years several hundred people had settled in and around Tiger. With increased numbers of people came new discoveries. In the decade that followed new claims like the Cashier and IxL lodes were found and registered. On July 20, 1872, the tireless George Read and D. W. Willey went prospecting for a third time. In company with Corydon Smith they found the St. Cloud Mine, a property that subsequently became one of the three greatest producers in the district. No less of a contribution was the consolidation of the Tiger and Tiger Extension into the Royal Tiger Mines Corporation.

During all of its life as a mining community, Tiger's most severe problem was the weather. Any time after mid-October, tarnished clouds begin spilling snow onto the cabins below, casting a hibernating slumber over the valley. Until late April or early May, chokingly fine snows swirl down from the heavens with virtually no warning. Early residents complained that it snowed most of the year at Tiger, a completely inaccurate statement. The summers were and still are delightful. Ore from the mines at Tiger was shipped out on horse-drawn sleds during the long winters.

In more recent times, dredges have worked the Swan Valley from nearly every angle. Many of Tiger's buildings that were adjacent to the river now lie under tons of smoothly-polished boulders. Farther up the hill, along both sides of

Courtesy Library, State Historical Society of Colorado
The old town of Tiger, on the Swan River

Collection of Robert L. Brown
Some of Tiger's old buildings still stand

the present road, some of the original buildings that survived still stand. Today, Tiger is very simple to find and the graded roads are in excellent condition. Start at Frisco and drive toward Breckenridge on State Highway 9. When you cross the Swan River, turn left onto the dirt road that runs east. Tiger is just five miles up this road.

59.

VULCAN

WEST OF GUNNISON and south of today's U.S. Highway 50, stands the crater of an ancient and now-extinct volcano. It was called Vulcan Hill for the Roman god of fire. Nearby, not far below the sagebrush-dotted surface, the so-called Great Gunnison County Gold Belt lay waiting to be tapped. When the gold was first discovered in 1895 a shantytown called Camp Creek sprang to life. Later, the name was changed to Vulcan.

Two years later, in 1897, there were 500 people in town and one newspaper, called the *Vulcan Enterprize.* Between 1900 and 1902, the short lived *Vulcan Times* was published by Robert and Rufus Crosby. School was held for five months each year. An old store building served as the classroom. Saturday night dances were held in the town with some regularity. But in 1907 there were still only 500 people there.

Two bits of excitement sparked the normally routine way of life at Vulcan. In May of 1899 the post office was robbed. Later that same year a siege of Union troubles upset the town. Affairs reached their peak when Union members locked up other miners, the superintendent and the bookkeeper in a bunkhouse. Armed guards prevented their departure. In a wild melee that followed one man was shot in the wrist and in the lung and the bookkeeper was severely beaten. To climax the whole affair, the non-Union men were marched at gunpoint through 12 miles of heavy snow to Iola.

When 20 Unionists were arrested and charged, a sympathetic jury found them "not guilty." Then all went out to celebrate with the booze juggler at a local saloon which boasted that its products were guaranteed to produce, "1,000 songs and 100 fights to the barrel." When rumors of British and French investments in Vulcan's mines swept the town, there was a mild flurry in building lot sales, but somehow it never materialized. During much of the time settlement bragging was the principal occupation, with the hope that population figures might rise above the rather irritating total of 500 people.

While some residents sat around counting their chickens before they were hatched, others got out and dug mine shafts. The ores here consisted of sulphur mixed with gold. Some closely located properties merged. After joining forces, the Lincoln, Vulcan and Good Hope mines produced a half million in gold. The Vulcan once had an underground fire that burned for several days.

In 1895 the St. Patrick and Mammoth Chimney mines were discovered. The latter property acquired its name from a natural 400 foot deep chimney that descended for some 400 feet vertically into the earth. Miners who worked down there sometimes called it "Gunnison County's deepest underground lunatic asylum." Later the Mammoth Chimney was consolidated with the Vulcan and Good Hope properties into the Vulcan Mines and Smelter Company.

When the Black Copper group of mines was first discovered, promising quartz and sulphide ores were shipped to the mills. Prior to their first collapse, some $400,000 in gold and silver was mined. About 200 men worked there and two loads of ore went to the smelter each week. Then in the winter of 1904-05 the deposits were seemingly exhausted and the whole operation came to a grinding halt. A rich deposit of copper was uncovered in the same shaft late in the summer of 1905, and a second boom began. Seemingly the deposits were endless and the owners erected a 40 ton smelter during the au-

Vulcan, on the Gunnison County gold belt

Vulcan had several buildings in 1969

tumn. Regrettably their optimism was unjustified. The copper leads played out and the whole community started to die.

More than half a century has passed now since the last Vulcanite left the town. Nevertheless, many of the old buildings are still there. To see them, drive west from Gunnison on U.S. Highway 50 for 10 miles to Iola. Turn south here on State Highway 149 and drive about 4 miles. At this point an unnumbered dirt road branches off to the southeast, left for 12 dusty miles to Vulcan. Most current maps show the above route.

An easier way to find Vulcan has appeared since the new dam was completed. Forget about Iola. Drive west from Gunnison on the same U.S. Highway 50 to the point where the new road to Powderhorn and Lake City crosses the reservoir over the new bridge. Turn south (left) here. Go for about one mile to the first left turn beyond the bridge. Turn onto this dirt road. It goes east for a short distance, then turns south and leads directly into Vulcan.

There are several ghost ranches along the way and several roads which branch off. Stay on the most-used road at all times. Vulcan can be identified from the accompanying photographs. The huge dumps on the hill above the town and to your right as you enter, are those of the Mammoth Chimney (extreme right) and Vulcan mines, whose dumps have now merged into a single pile.

60.

WARD

VIEWED IN RETROSPECT, Ward started earlier and has lasted far longer than most of its contemporaries among Colorado mining camps. Established in 1860, the first settlement at this location was called Columbia or sometimes Columbia City. Later, of course, the name was changed to honor Calvin W. Ward who discovered the Miser's Dream Mine in the spring of 1860, the first discovery to be made on the great underground mineral complex that was soon to be known as the Ward lode. Ward's find was in Indiana Gulch, a branch of Left Hand Creek, at a point 18 miles northwest of Boulder, six miles above booming Gold Hill, and eight miles north of the later site of Caribou.

Although some other precious metals were found in its mines, Ward was known primarily as a gold camp. Within a few months Cyrus W. Deardoff had located the Columbia, Utica, Baxter, Idaho, and Boston. From the Ni Wot the owners took $100,000 in loose surface gold which they reduced in a crude stamp mill. During its early years alone, the Ni Wot yielded $700,000, mostly in gold. In 1888, H. A. W. Tabor bought the Ni Wot mine for an undisclosed price and began operating it through his Tabor Investment Company of Denver. Tabor soon authorized construction of two 50 stamp mills for crushing the ore from the Ni Wot. Among other notable mines of the district were the Stougthon, Celestial, Humboldt, and the White Raven, which also produced lead in paying quantities.

And around these rich mines, a town grew up, 9,250 feet above sea level. In the early years, the population hovered around 400 people. By 1865, 600 people lived there. Most of the usual kinds of business establishments were represented at Ward. In addition, there were also a fire house and a jail, both of which are still standing. A newspaper, the *Ward Miner*, was published for a while. Ward finally incorporated itself on June 9, 1896.

Then in 1910 came that nearly inevitable scourge of high country mining camps, the fire. On January 24, a smudge in an ash can behind the McClancy Hotel got out of hand. Fanned by a high wind, it burned for 6 hours. Fifty-three buildings, valued at $85,000 were destroyed. Insurance covered only $7,500 of the loss. Residents doused both the school and the two churches with water, saving these structures from the flames. Ward's Congregational and Catholic churches were both completed in 1896. Although the Congregationalists still use their building for services, the Catholic church has now become a garage.

Transportation to Ward was always fairly good. In the early days a stagecoach road ran over Sawmill Hill to Gold Hill and on to Ward. George Crofutt in his *Grip-Sack Guide of Colorado* listed this as Post Road No. 8. The fare from Boulder was $6.00. In its entirety, 40 miles of roads were used for this run. Stages made the trip 6 times weekly during the Ward boom. Passengers could leave Boulder at 8:00 A.M., arriving at Ward by 8:00 P.M. the next evening.

Just before the turn of the present century, Ward got a railroad too. The Colorado and Northwestern, the narrow gauge mining line was planned in 1897. All of the stock was owned and controlled by a board of 7 men. Popularly, this enterprise was frequently referred to as the Whiplash Route, for the rather obvious side effects of its many loops and sharp turns. Completed in June of 1898, the Colorado and Northwestern played a significant role in the mining development of Boulder County, bringing a stream of hu-

Much of Ward still remains

manity into a whole series of the more remote towns that had grown up in the mountains around Ward.

On June 23, 1898, the first narrow gauge locomotive and a few cars passed over the newly laid tracks. Five days later they were open for business. When the first train pulled into Ward, the principal streets of the town had been decked out with ornamental bunting and crepe paper decorations. Governor Alva Adams rode in the first coach, lending an air of dignity to the festivities. Business was good almost from the start. On the average, Ward's mines shipped about 100 tons of ore daily. In its passenger coaches, the railroad carried 250 passengers on most days. When the decline came and the tracks were torn out, the railroad station became a little store on the hillside above Ward. It still serves the community in this same capacity today.

Although it has seen better days, Ward is still alive today, with many of its original buildings spread out across the meadow below the Peak to Peak Highway. Below the town, visitors may still see the original stone constructed Utica Mill, which was powered by water, piped to the refinery from a site over the mountains 5 miles away. From State Highway No. 7, north of Boulder, turn left or west on the Left Hand Canyon road to Ward. An alternate route involves using State Highway No. 160 north from Nederland or south from Raymond. Either route will carry you to Ward.

Courtesy Library, State Historical Society of Colorado
An old photograph of Ward. The Catholic church is at lower right

Collection of Robert L. Brown
*Ward as it looked in the summer of 1964. The school is at upper
left and the hotel is left of the center.*

61.

WEBSTER

WEBSTER WAS A TOUGH, typical, end-of-the-tracks railroad town. It was started as a tent city by drifters and adventurers who were on their way to Leadville. The Denver, South Park, and Pacific Railroad had reached the foot of Kenosha Hill in January of 1879. During the early years of the Leadville excitement, this was as far as one could go on the coaches. From this point, stages and wagons met the train and carried passengers and freight over Kenosha into South Park.

Kenosha Pass is a mere 9,950 feet high. Its name came from Kenosha, Wisconsin. During its stagecoach period, it was sometimes referred to as Kenosha Summit. Today it is a paved road, a part of U.S. Highway No. 285. In later years, after the railroad had topped its crest, the name Kenosha Station was used to describe the railroad facilities which included a station house, water tank and siding that grew up there.

Actually, the town of Webster was a shipping point at the foot of two passes. In addition to Kenosha, there was also a Webster Pass, the real source of the town's name. One year earlier, in 1878, William and Emerson Webster had entered into a partnership with the Montezuma Silver Mining Company. The purpose of this association was to construct a shorter, more convenient road that would enable mining, freight and passenger traffic to move in and out of the Peru Creek and Snake River mining districts. When completed,

Webster Pass shortened the long trek out by way of the remote Georgia Pass and South Park. Its chief advantage and popularity were directly attributable to the fact that it got up over the mountains on the eastern or Denver side of Kenosha Pass.

Thus in an incredibly short time, the Webster crossing became the chief freighting and stagecoach route from Denver to the Snake River towns. At its apex, Webster Pass was 12,108 feet high where it crossed the Continental Divide. The Rev. John L. (Father) Dyer, most energetic of the Methodist circuit riders, often used Webster Pass, and persistent rumors still survive describing how he may have staked a mining claim on the side of nearby Collier Mountain.

In both the 1880 and in the rare 1885 editions of his *Grip-Sack Guide of Colorado,* George Crofutt described the stagecoach trip over the top by Post Road out of Webster. Driving west, it passed through Hall Valley and Handcart Gulch on the eastern side before crossing the range. Quite apart from its correct designation, Webster Pass was sometimes popularly known as Handcart or Montezuma Pass. Dropping down from the top, the more gradual grades carried the coaches into Montezuma, Saints John and Preston. From the Snake River towns, passengers could make other connections for Peru Creek or could continue on up over the mountains again, finally reaching Lincoln City and Breckenridge. Travelers could leave Webster thrice weekly, on Mondays, Wednesdays or Fridays, at 7:00 A.M., arriving at Breckenridge by 6:00 P.M. the following day. The difficulties of this trip may be better appreciated when it is pointed out that it took a bone-jarring 36 hours to get over these 39 long miles to Breckenridge in the early 1880s.

When the Denver, South Park, and Pacific Railroad reached Webster, a station and water tank were erected. The fare from Denver was $7.00 each way. In later years there were two passenger trains daily, one from the east and another from the west. At that time Webster had the reputation of being a very rough town. Two cemeteries, one a "Boot Hill" type, survive to prove it. Both are above the highway on the right side as you drive west toward Kenosha Pass. Although Webster was not essentially a mining town, it served the nearby Hall Valley and Geneva Mining districts. Entering the town from the east, a long row of coke ovens once stood beside the road. Presumably they supplied coke for the Hall Valley and other smelters.

One incident described by George Crofutt will illustrate the rawness of Webster's frontier environment. Here, the hapless traveler with an overnight lay-over could purchase sleep space on the floor of the town's only "hotel." For the rate of $1.00 per body, the benevolent proprietor offered the use of a blanket. On those occasions when the demand exceeded the supply, the furtive landlord watched carefully for a sound sleeper and stealthily snatched away the covering. Quite often the same blanket would be resold many times during the long hours of a single night. In fact, the proprietor regarded it as a "poor night" when the same blanket could only be sold 3 or 4 times.

Webster began to die when the railroad gots its tracks up over Kenosha Hill and better accommodations and connections became available elsewhere. Webster today is a pathetic shadow of its former self, with a few empty shells still surviving beside the Kenosha Pass road. From this point on U.S. Highway No. 285, at the eastern foot of the pass, the old dirt road still goes west up to Hall Valley and toward the currently impossible crossing of Webster Pass, above Handcart Gulch. Many 4-wheel-drive enthusiasts, including the writer, have attempted to find the original road from Montezuma, Saints Johns and Preston, over to Lincoln City and Breckenridge. Alas, how they got over the second range is still a mystery. At this writing, a lush growth of trees has made even an approximate determination of this route difficult. In the meantime, Webster has taken its place among the almost-forgotten boom towns of early Colorado.

Courtesy Library, State Historical Society of Colorado
Here was Webster in a more prosperous time

Collection of Robert L. Brown
Many of Webster's original structures are still there

62.

WESTCLIFFE

SPANISH EXPLORERS HAD PENETRATED Colorado's great upland parks and many of its high valleys a full century or more
prior to the arrival of fur traders and gold seekers. But in
most cases they failed to conquer the peaks or to unlock the
great treasure chests buried there. The narcotic craving for
quick riches led to the establishment of several communities in the beautiful Wet Mountain Valley. One of the last
of these was Westcliffe, formerly known as Clifton. Nearby
Silver Cliff, 1½ miles away, was started in 1878. Both neighboring towns shared a common altitude of 7,800 feet above
sea level, here at the eastern edge of the storm-facing bosom
of the Sangre de Cristo mountains. Geologically, this range
is regarded as the youngest in the Rockies, with 8 summits
that pierce the sky with altitudes in excess of 14,000 feet.

Dr. J. W. Bell first entered the Wet Mountain Valley with
Gen. William J. Palmer of the Denver and Rio Grande Railroad in 1870. He returned to help start the town of Clifton.
Later, it was known as West Cliff, spelled as two words (see
inset photograph of trade token). Bell kited the name from
his European birthplace, Westcliffe-on-Sea, England. Although life went on here prior to formal founding, the actual
legal beginnings date from 1885. Grandiose and colorful
tales to the contrary notwithstanding, Westcliffe owed its
beginnings and growth to the D.&R.G. Railroad. It was an
end-of-tracks town, the terminus of the so-called Silver
Cliff branch which had been completed in 1881. In May of

that year, the Grape Creek line of the D.&R.G. was finished from Canon City to Westcliffe. It did not go on to Silver Cliff, despite its popular name. Instead, the track layers stopped short of Silver Cliff to increase land values at that point. A stagecoach line connected the two towns.

After 1882, many Silver Cliff families began moving to Westcliffe as mining started into one of its periodic declines. Another rather compelling reason was the promise of lower taxes held out by the newer town. Some residents uprooted their homes off old foundations and moved them up the road to Westcliffe. Most of the paying mines that had provided the original impetus for settlement were over at Silver Cliff. Included among them were such properties as the Plata Verde, Island City, Lady Franklin, Alta Verde, Crescent, Vanderbilt, Songbird, St. Mary's, Terrible, Rambler, Milkmaid, and Bull Domingo. Residents from both of the towns worked in the deep shafts that penetrated the great mineralized cliff beside the town.

In 1886 a battle for the county seat developed. Westcliffe and Silver Cliff joined forces to wrest the coveted designation from the reluctant Rosita. A vigilante committee was formed in the two towns. Members of this extra-legal society labored like evangelists at a revival altar. With gargantuan optimism they entered Rosita and forcibly divested the official documents and records from the confused city officials. Once the deed had been accomplished, a new courthouse was erected. To assure future peace, this latest civic edifice was put up on a site halfway between Silver Cliff and Westcliffe. As time passed, so did the county seat designation. Westcliffe eventually won it away from Silver Cliff and still holds the distinction at this writing. Quite apart from the founding date, Westcliffe was not actually incorporated until 1897.

Over the years Westcliffe has had its ups and downs. But tragedy is not always veiled in black. It sometimes assumes very watery proportions. A swift-striking storm swirled

Collection of Fred and Jo Mazulla
Westcliffe in 1894, with a flood raging down its main street. Poor horse!

Collection of Robert L. Brown
Westcliffe in 1967, the busy seat of Custer County. Inset shows early trade token from West Cliff.

out of the heavens on August 17 and 18, 1889. Tarnished gray clouds spilled a hard, driving rain on the valley below. The ensuing flood out of Grape Creek outroared the wind with a plunging cannonade of water and mud that ripped out the D.&R.G. tracks in 5 short minutes. From then on the company regarded further maintenance of the line to Westcliffe as hopeless. In 1900 the route was abandoned and the rails torn out.

Westcliffe today is one of the most spectacularly situated of Colorado villages. Its population hovers around the 300 mark, with income from agriculture, stock raising and hay ranching. To see it, drive south from Texas Creek on U.S. Highway No. 50 for about 21 miles on State Highway No. 69 to the town. State highways No. 67 and No. 96 south and west out of Florence will also carry you there.

63.

WHITEHORN

ALTHOUGH A VARIETY of aboriginal Americans had penetrated Colorado's vast mountain-ringed upland meadows at least a full century before the coming of mining men, their culturally induced preoccupation with such pursuits as hunting buffalo and fighting each other largely precluded any chance for the establishment of permanent settlements. Beginning in 1859, hundreds of remote towns grew up to house the hordes of gold and silver seekers who came to Colorado. Even though the practice of mining had begun to decline, some new communities were still coming into existence in the late 1890s. One of these was Whitehorn, founded in May of 1897, and named for A. L. Whitehorn, the original locator. In another version a prospector named Dennis Patno found the Independence lode in February of 1897, thus precipitating a rush into the district.

Almost immediately, Whitehorn sold his gold claims to the Cameron Mines Land and Tunnel Company and took a job with the new owners, looking after company business. Shortly after they had gained title to the claims, the Cameron people laid out a town and erected a variety of buildings. By December of 1898 some 600 persons were living at Whitehorn and there was a brand new telephone line that had been extended in from Salida, 15 miles away. About 2,000 persons lived in the whole district, including the towns of Turret and Calumet. In just over a year, the Whitehorn area had changed from a grazing and timber economy to a growing mining camp. Both timber and water were available in abundance. By the end of 1898, some 800 persons lived there and lots sold for $500 each. Whitehorn's altitude is 8,500 feet high.

One newspaper account, published in December of 1898, reported 150-200 occupied dwellings at Whitehorn. At least one boardinghouse and a 10 room hotel also flourished. Inevitably, there was also a saloon, in addition to 3 general stores, a livery stable and one newspaper, the *Whitehorn News*. The *Denver Times* reported 1,000 residents at Whitehorn in November of 1898 and a stagecoach line began coming in from Salida. Another good stagecoach road connected the town with Newett. Each morning at 9:30 A.M., the coach left for Whitehorn. Passengers could connect with Colorado Midland trains No. 5 and No. 6 when they arrived at Newett by noon. At 4:00 P.M. each afternoon a return coach started back, arriving at Whitehorn by 7:00 P.M. On May 23, 1899, a mail contract was awarded to George H. Trader for the purpose of carrying letters and packages from Salida to Whitehorn. For this service, Trader was paid $893 per year.

Inevitably, outside capital heard about Whitehorn and came to invest. From Cripple Creek, Frank M. and Harry E. Woods, owners of the far-flung empire known as the Woods Investment Company, came and bought up 70 claims in the neighborhood of Whitehorn. On November 14, 1898, the Woods brothers put 40 men and their teams onto the job of doing something to beautify Whitehorn. A contract was made with the Cameron Mines, Land and Tunnel Company to macadamize 2 miles of both Main Street and Chora Avenue. Using 18 inches of crushed rock as a base, the completed streets were to be 80 feet wide. These streets would be new ones, not a part of the original plat. In the facelifting process, many buildings were moved or turned on their foundations to increase the beauty of the town. In all, 10 blocks were graded and new sidewalks were laid. The completed townsite covered a level tract of about 100 acres.

These cabins at Whitehorn were among the few to survive the big fire of 1902

One of the rewards for the quiet watcher on back-country trails

In the foothills area south of the town mining claims covered some 1,000 acres. Since Colorado mining districts were rather small, two seem to have been required to fill the bill. These were the Cameron and the Cleora districts. Although the mines were mainly gold producers, some copper was also found. Most of the ores from those districts assayed out at $3,000 to the ton. In 1898 there were only 3 ore shippers, but this number increased sharply within a relatively short time. The quality and quantity of free gold soon impressed the inspectors who came up from Cripple Creek. Although there was only one mill in the town, a rotary stamp affair with a capacity of 30 tons per day, there was a full-fledged smelter down the hill at Salida, only 15 miles away.

In the beginning there were plans for operating the whole district with one main tunnel, from which numerous branches would lead off to the several mines. As the district grew, the impracticality of this concept soon became apparent. For example, the previously mentioned Woods brothers held a total of those 70 claims in the name of their Woods Investment Company. For a start, the Woods people spent $50,000 in improving their properties. Beyond this, a variety of other properties flourished. The Molly Gibson, discovered in December of 1898 and owned by the Cameron Mines, Land and Tunnel Company, was not far from town. Father Malone of Denver owned the U. P. lode. The Guess was located on Hayden Mountain. Other notable properties that contributed to the economy of Whitehorn were the Ida, Dunn-Litts, Ethel Rivers, Eureka, Bull Quartz, Emma, King Solomon, Byefield, Golden Island No. 1 and No. 2, Dunkard, June Bug, Cleopatra, Rosewood Casket, Independence, Golden Eagle, Prairie, Little Rose, Whitehorn, and the Corinne Group. A few, like the Anaconda, were named for notable Cripple Creek properties.

If contemporary estimates were at all correct, nearly all Colorado mining camps were swept at least once by disastrous conflagrations. Whitehorn's ordeal by fire came at the close of a fine spring day in 1902. The exact date was May 24, and the time was 9:00 P.M. at the Witting Hotel, a defective flue in one of the stoves had gone unnoticed until it was too late. Outside, a stiff wind came swirling down from the heavens with a directionless blast. Quickly the flames spread to the roof, outroaring the wind for a time, spewing a cannonade of plunging sparks onto the surrounding buildings below. Nearly everything the frantic miners attempted failed to contain the angry blazing inferno. In quick succession the fire consumed the hotel, general store, lumber yard, and Cresswell Brothers and Cochrans saloon. During the height of the confusion Mr. Witting was severely injured.

Although the post office and the telephone building escaped unscathed, about half of the town was destroyed. In an account printed in the *Denver Republican* on May 25, 1902, the following day, it was reported that "Mrs. A. A. Lampa of Whitehorn was prostrated by the sight of her home burning, but is now recovering."

Measured by the standards of its time, Whitehorn was a fairly typical mining town and passed through the usual phases indigenous to such places. Little was done to refurbish the town after the fire. Over the years most of the remaining cabins have collapsed, one by one. Only a few are still standing at this writing. To see them, start from the oil storage tanks on the northern edge of Salida. Take the dirt road that leads off through San Isabel National Forest toward the northeast. At this writing the forks are marked and the road, although rough, is passable all the way. At the only important intersection turn right. The left fork goes to Turret. The Whitehorn road, State Highway No. 189, climbs over and around a succession of rolling, aspen-clad hillsides for about 7 more miles. Whitehorn's remains are there, below the road on the right side in a broad meadow just below the crest of a hill. If followed, this same road goes on and enters South Park by way of a pleasant, winding but circuitous route. Some years ago the Whitehorn townsite was purchased by a man from Ohio. Since the old site is fenced, courtesy dictates that you secure permission before exploring the old town.

64.

WINFIELD

QUITE A VARIETY of names were attached to this town before it finally settled down to be just plain Winfield. Although it achieved its greatest fame, such as it was, during the Cripple Creek boom, there were settlers here for more than a full decade prior to the great gold discoveries near Mt. Pisgah. When the first post office was authorized on April 1, 1880, the settlement was known as Summit or Summit Park. When George Crofutt passed through the camp a few years later, he referred to the mail facility as a "Ranch post office up on the Ute Pass wagon road." Crofutt also remarked upon the abundant game and trout available nearby.

The *Colorado Business Directory* for 1886 and 1887 listed Summit and showed a population of thirty people. There was no mention of mining at that time. In the files of the Library of the Colorado State Historical Society, a notation appears suggesting that the early name came from the fact that Summit was built on the summit of a mountain. Actually it is on the top of Globe Hill, one of the prominences that now overlooks the city of Cripple Creek. To further establish the location, it was a half mile north from Midway, at an elevation of 9,918 feet above sea level. All things considered, it was a sleepy little farm village during this earlier existence. Prior to 1896, all mail came up from Manitou Springs. After that date, postal deliveries were routed up from Fountain.

Everything in this timberline hayfield changed after Bob

Womack found the first gold in December of 1890. With the increased number of migrants who entered the region, Summit became a station on the Colorado Midland Railroad. After 1900, the Colorado Springs and Cripple Creek District Railroad had extended their lines up into the basin by way of one of the most scenic rides in America. This railroad was more often called the Short Line. When Teddy Roosevelt rode up to Cripple Creek via the Short Line in 1901 he made the often repeated remark about how the scenery along the way bankrupted the English language. The railroad also maintained a passing track and a wooden telegraph office at Summit Park. Summit was the highest point on the line.

Here, the railroad also maintained an eating house for their passengers. For those who were not hungry, there was plenty of time to enjoy the magnificent view of the Sangre de Cristo Mountains off to the west. Beyond them, on a clear day, visitors could see the La Sal Range in eastern Utah. From Summit, one could always anticipate the long, thrilling ride back down the steep grades with majestic valleys and the eastern plains spread out below. Sometimes the engineer would get carried away with it all. The C.S.&C.C.D. management once fired an engineer for running too fast downgrade between Summit and Duffields.

In its next phase of life, Summit was purchased and subsequently taken over by Winfield Scott Stratton, best known and most eccentric of the several millionaires who emerged from the Cripple Creek excitement. In this period, the town was known variously as Stratton, Strattonia and finally as Winfield, its official name on contemporary maps. This town should not be confused with the other Winfield south and west of Leadville, which was also named for this most remarkable man.

Under Mr. Stratton, office buildings were added to the collection of shanties which had been put up at the site to house those families that worked at the nearby Logan, Anchoria, and American Eagle mines. Using this as his headquarters,

Stratton managed and expanded his extensive holdings in the "Bowl of Gold." With Pike's Peak as a backdrop, this was a magnificent and entirely appropriate location for the headquarters of the man who became known as the "Midas of the Rockies."

The career of Stratton as a personality, from migratory carpenter to one of the richest mining kings of the west, is almost stranger than fiction. By this time, the facts and legends of his life have become so intricately interwoven that it would be an insuperable task to sort them out. Among the few people who penetrated Stratton's veneer of suspicion, loneliness and mistrust, there is no middle ground of opinion. Those who knew him well became either staunch friends who could see no evil, or bitter enemies who could see no good.

He prospected at Red Cliff, Leadville, in the Sangre de Cristos, at Tin Cup, around Aspen and in the San Juans. Each winter he worked as a carpenter in order to finance his annual prospecting activities when summer rolled around. Each new discovery attracted him like the proverbial pot of gold at the end of a rainbow. For nearly two decades he sought the rich mineral deposits but to no avail.

In 1891, his luck changed. On July 3, he had put down his camp roll at an obscure spot on Battle Mountain, above present-day Victor. A much-repeated story tells how Sratton had a particularly vivid dream that night about finding gold, a not too unlikely subject considering his obsession. Upon awakening on Independence Day, memories of his nocturnal preoccupation were still so vivid that he dashed off without drinking his breakfast to file a claim on the unlikely-looking ledge beside his campsite. The eventual result was the great Independence Mine which was later sold for $11,-000,000. Stratton himself got $10,000,000, with the rest going as the agent's commission to Verner Z. Reed. Nearby he found the nearly equally rich Washington property.

With the passage of time he bought out something over one hundred other claims. These holdings were incorporated into the Stratton Cripple Creek Mining and Development company which had its headquarters at Winfield. His driving ambition now became the outright ownership of the entire bowl of gold. He theorized that the erupting volcano, which had put gold into this basin, had a central vortex, like the post of an umbrella. From this, like ribs on the umbrella, the gold deposits had radiated out. Stratton drew up a map showing how these ribs had surfaced around the rim of the Bowl of Gold to become the great mines of the Cripple Creek District. All of these, he was sure, had come from one great central molten cauldron which he expected to find deep inside Pike's Peak, at about the level of the plains. After much study and speculation about the relative positions of the richest veins, Stratton decided on a tract of land that theoretically should be directly above the central core of pure gold. Stealthily he bided his time, buying every claim that appeared on the market until, at last, he owned the coveted piece of land at the center.

Shortly afterward, he supervised the drilling of a 1,000-foot-deep shaft. When it was done, he expected it to extend for more than a mile straight down. Record size timbers were cut to order and shipped in to reinforce the walls. Unfortunately Stratton was not a temperate man. His daily liquor consumption was staggering in more ways than one. In this, as in so many similar cases, he died of cirrhosis of the liver. After his death in September of 1902, the plan to find the vortex of gold collapsed. No other mining company with adequate capital has cared to gamble on the Stratton theory.

To date, several books have been written detailing Winfield Scott Stratton's many eccentricities. Among other things he mistrusted preachers and hated lawyers. Although he was by no means indifferent to feminine charms, he sampled the institution of matrimony only once, and that briefly. During the remainder of his short life he maintained a virtual harem within the several hotels scattered throughout the Cripple Creek District and pursued a truly bacchanalian

Winfield was beautifully situated on the top of Globe Hill

Behind Winfield, at left, Pikes Peak is clearly visible

existence. He suspected the motives of any woman who ever broached the subject of matrimony to him.

On the other hand he was kind and generous to a fault. His great wealth attracted every scheming jackal in the business. Despite his avowed repugnance toward the clergy, he once gave Father Volpe a most generous sum for his church in Gillett. Stratton, by the way, was a Mason. In one winter alone he shelled out $83,000 for the Salvation Army to feed and clothe the unemployed. When he found that laundresses in Colorado Springs could not afford carfare, he bought bicycles for all young ladies employed in the several laundries. He set up men in the carpentry business and secretly bought horses and surreys for many indigents too old or feeble to work. His entire life was a paradox.

The decline of Winfield paralleled the decline of the whole Cripple Creek District. By 1913, it was already a ghost town. By 1922, all of the rolling stock of the Colorado Springs and Cripple Creek District Railroad, the Short Line, had been sold. Later, of course, even the tracks were torn out. However, the old grades were retained, regraded, and became the Corley Highway. It is now referred to as the Gold Camp Road, one of the most beautiful rides in the state when the aspens are yellow. Due to its remote location, a wire fence, and several rather blunt signs about trespassing, much of Winfield remains. Several big brick structures and a larger number of smaller frame homes are still standing at the site.

U.S. Highway 24 enters the mountains west of Colorado Springs and climbs up past Woodland Park to Divide. Here, State Highway 67 cuts south toward Cripple Creek. After passing the site of Gillett, the road bends around and drops into the basin of the old volcano. From this points, on top of the hill, a dirt road goes left. If you prefer, start down into the basin and turn left beside the Molly Kathleen Mine. This road, and the one from on top of the hill, intersect. Follow this good graded road to the top of Globe Hill. At the top, a slight detour into the trees to your right will take you to Winfield. Since most of the town is visible from the fence, common courtesy demands that you do not trespass without permission. Winfield is deserted now and much of it is tinder dry. A heedless act could destroy it. Winfield was a model town, dedicated to the memory of a most unusual man.

65.

YANKEE HILL

BY TODAY'S STANDARDS, the building of a town on the top of cold, wind-swept, barren Yankee Hill seems as out of place as putting a cow on the front porch. There are frosts nearly every night on this high prominence which divides Clear Creek County from Gilpin County. Although the much-used wagon and stagecoach road from Central City to Georgetown traversed Yankee Hill at a much earlier time, little serious thought was given to the mining potential of the area until rich gold float was found there, near the sur-face, in the 1890s. Beginning then, a tent city started to take form, housing some 200 persons who had come to con-quer the peaks and to unlock any great treasure chest that might lie buried there. Within four to five months, the tent city had virtually disappeared as large numbers of log cabins were erected.

Both the hill and the town that later grew up on it were named by northern sympathizers during the Civil War. As a community, Yankee Hill was known as a peaceful, law abiding place. Although Central City was only 7 miles away, the men preferred to brawl in Denver once a month, on pay day. Only one saloon, a small one, ever flourished at Yankee Hill. While this would seem to present a sociological para-dox, research has failed to turn up any alternative informa-tion beyond the fact that the beer glasses in the local saloon were small while the Denver booze jugglers served their product in 36 ounce glasses. The pay of a miner at this time

This was the original town of Yankee Hill

The high, windswept expanse of Yankee Hill today

was not great. With seeming pride in the character reputations they enjoyed at home, the men of Yankee Hill did their carousing in the gin mills, love stores and gambling halls of Denver. Yankee Hill itself was always a peaceful place.

For the pioneer who settled at Yankee Hill, there was a magnificent view of Saint Mary's Glacier and the front range. Because of its altitude, the hill was nearly always a very cold place in winter. During one particularly bad period, a blizzard started on April 22, 1902, and the stagecoach, carrying both mail and passengers, was 5 hours late. When the coach finally pulled in at Yankee Hill, the driver was actually coated with ice.

After some initial slowness, an electric line was finally extended to Yankee Hill by way of Fall River Canyon. Its wires reached the town on July 28, 1902, financed for some reason by the Burlington Railroad Company. Almost exactly a year later the Colorado Telephone Company ran its wires up to the town from the other side. From Black Hawk, the lines were installed to Apex and then across the mountains for the last 7 miles to Yankee Hill. To facilitate shipment of ore to the refineries at Idaho Springs, work was done on the road through Alice and Fall River Canyon, beginning in 1905. Long before the arrival of these socially desirable improvements, the *Denver Times* for July 21, 1899, reported that all cabins at Yankee Hill were full. In addition to privately owned dwellings, some of the mining companies also put up quarters of one sort or another to shelter their unmarried workers. The North Star Mine had a fine, large boardinghouse. Captain H. I. Seeman of the Yankee Consolidated Company had several cabins "suitable for occupancy by married miners and their families." Single men who were employed by the same company were taken care of in one of the boardinghouses, run by private parties.

Yankee Hill was located within the boundaries of the Northwest Lincoln Mining District. Financial backing for the many mines came principally from New York, Ohio,

Pennsylvania and California capitalists. Here as elsewhere, a mining association was organized at a rather early stage of the town's life.

On May 14, 1900, the *Denver Republican* reported the formation of this group in order to fight claim jumpers and to advertise the camp. This latter goal was probably conceived in desperation, since very little paying ore was actually taken out in proportion to the vast amounts of money invested there.

It was thought for a time that a road to the smelters at Idaho Springs would result in prosperity through shorter and less costly hauling of unrefined ores to the mills. The previously mentioned Fall River road had been improved with this in mind. But a majority of the absentee owners and managers seem to have lived in Gilpin County rather than in Clear Creek County. As a result most of the refining was done at the more distant Black Hawk installations.

Despite these seemingly insurmountable odds, a rather amazing number of mining ventures tried to make a go of it at Yankee Hill. The Gold Anchor was turning out ores worth $600.00 to the ton at one time, but not for long. While boisterously counting their chickens before they were hatched, the Gold Anchor people built their own concentrator in 1905. The nearby Pioneer Mill, erected according to the same sort of speculation, was a 5 stamp operation. Great improvements were also planned by Captain H. I. Seeman, president and manager of the Yankee Consolidated Mining, Milling and Tunneling Company. He hoped to erect a new shaft house on the rich Lombard property which produced ores worth $400.00 to the ton. A horse-powered boiler, an air compressor, and new drills were purchased. This company employed between 50 and 100 men at the Lombard. It owned about 80 properties around Yankee Hill. A few of the Consolidated holdings were silver producers. Captain Seeman had his own company-owned assay office in the town.

According to the *Daily News* of March 16, 1899, a one-fourth interest in the Stone Wall mine was sold to Denver parties for $2,000. A company was quickly formed with $10,000 in working capital. Although the camp had been inactive under adverse circumstances, the turn of the century brought a false boom that resulted in many old properties, idle for years, starting up with a lively work program. Among these were the Pay Dirt Mine, owned by a Dr. Shaw of Denver; the Seminole Group, made up of a group of 5 claims; the Eureka, owned by George Ebert of Denver; and the North Star, which was the property of Albert B. Sanford, also of Denver. A group of California men opened up the mines of Alice, just below Yankee Hill on the Fall River side. Between Alice and the top of the hill, the Ninety Four Tunnel was drilled and a small settlement grew up around it.

At the peak of the boom, three shifts were at work around the clock in the Manhattan Tunnel. Among mines in the district that became producers of a sort were the Portland No. 1, Klondyke Tunnel, Meadowlark, Isabella, Curfew, Chesapeake Tunnel, Cumberland, Faust, Pennsylvania, and the Surprise, owned by the Lincoln Mining Company.

With the passage of time, even the gargantuan optimism of the newspapers and of the professional promoters could not conceal the fact that mining futures at Yankee Hill left much to be desired. Within the span of the few years that the fever lasted, long hauls to the mills ate up too much of the profits from ores that were only moderately gold bearing anyway.

Only gnarled, rheumatic trees, acres of low-cut stumps, battered cabins and abandoned shafts mark the site of Yankee Hill today. There are at least two ways of getting there. Both require a 4-wheel-drive vehicle or a short hike. Taken as a whole, the Fall River side provides the easier access. From Interstate 70 just west of Idaho Springs, take the Fall River exit and follow this road to the ghost town of Alice. Although there are branches that leave this road, stay on the most used or main road. At Alice, a left turn beside two cabins would carry you into that town. Avoid this turn;

stay on the main road. Barely beyond this intersection, a less well traveled trail cuts across the ditch and branches steeply up the hill to your right. Take this trail, avoiding the two places where other trails fork off to the left. The second of these cut-offs goes to the Ninety Four Tunnel. You are now within a mile of Yankee Hill. From this point you should use a Jeep or get out and walk. Most people play it safe and walk from Alice, as the road becomes both steep and rocky beyond that point. From the trail to Ninety Four keep climbing on the well defined but rough trail up to the barren summit of Yankee Hill. In winter this is a favorite snowshoe trip of ours, but be prepared for both wind and cold.

The other but longer road follows the stagecoach route from the top of Cemetery Hill above Central City. At this writing, Forest Service markers will direct you from the cemeteries, but this is no road for conventional cars. As a Jeep road, this is not difficult. A couple of mildly precarious rock fills are the only problems. At the various forks, stay on the most traveled sets of ruts over the several miles to the town. Snow, even in summer, is no rarity on Yankee Hill.

INDEX

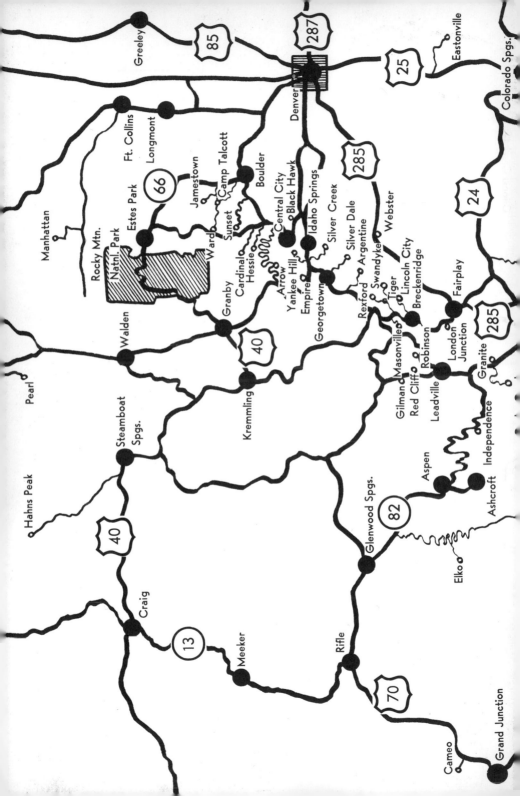